YPRES

AND

THE BATTLES OF YPRES

ITINERARY:

LILLE—ARMENTIÈRES—MESSINES—POELCAPPELLE

—YPRES—POPERINGHE—

LES MONTS—BAILLEUL—BÉTHUNE—LILLE.

Published by

MICHELIN & CIE.

Clermont-Ferrand, France.

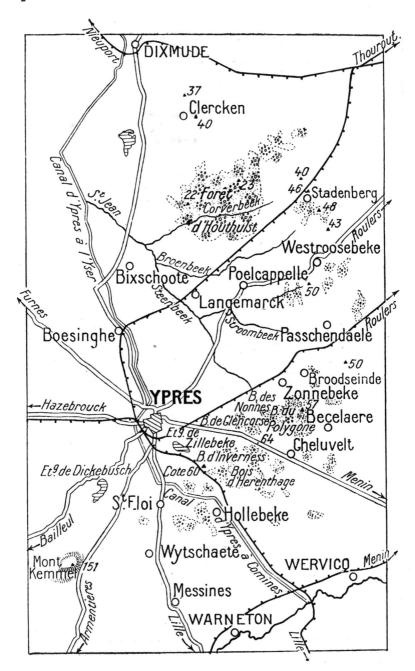

YPRES

AND THE BATTLES FOR ITS POSSESSION

FOREWORD

The town of Ypres lies in a sort of natural basin formed by a maritime plain intersected by canals, and dominated on the north, north-east and south by low wooded hills.

These canals, of which the Yser Canal is the most important, follow a general direction south-east—north-west. A number of streams flowing in the same direction also water the plain. In addition, there are the Dickebusch, Zillebeke and Bellewaarde ponds.

The hills forming the sides of this basin are very low and partly wooded. The line of their crests runs approximately from north to south, through Houthulst Forest (road from Poelcappelle to Clercken), Poelcappelle, Passchendaele, Broodseinde, Becelaere, Gheluvelt, the strategic Hill 60 (south of Zillebeke) and St. Eloi. Further south is the Messines-Wytschaete ridge, and to the south-west the Hills of Flanders.

Houthulst Forest is the largest of the woods. Next come the islets of Westroosebeke and Passchendaele, then, south of Zonnebeke, Polygone Wood, Nonne-Bosschen (or Nonnes) Wood, and the Woods of Glencorse, Inverness and Herenthage.

In this region, with its essentially maritime climate, the war assumed a character entirely different from that of the rest of the front. The marshy ground, almost at sea-level, is further sodden by constant rain and mists, and forms a spongy mass, in which it was impossible to dig trenches or underground shelters. Water is found immediately below the surface, so that the only possible defence-works were parapets. The bursting shells made huge craters which, promptly filling with water, became so many death-traps for wounded and unwounded alike.

The defence on both sides consequently centred around the woods, villages, and numerous farms, which were converted into redoubts with concrete blockhouses and deep wire entanglements. The slightest bits of rising ground here played an important part, and were fiercely disputed. The crests which dominate the basin of Ypres were used as observation-posts—the lowering sky being usually unfavourable for aerial observation—while their counter-slopes masked the concentrations of troops for the attacks.

It was therefore along the line of crests and around the fortified farms that the fighting reached its maximum of intensity.

The principal military operations which took place in the vicinity of the town between October, 1914, and November, 1917, may be divided as follows :—First, a powerful German offensive—a counter-stroke to the battles of the Yser—then a very definite effort to take the town. The *rôle* of the Allied armies was at that time purely defensive.

The second stage was marked by a British and Franco-British offensive, begun in the second half of 1916 and considerably developed during the summer and autumn of the following year. The object of these operations, which ended in November, 1917, was the clearing of Ypres. All the objectives were attained and the plains of Flanders were opened to the Allies.

A final effort by the Germans in great strength to the south of the town was checked by the resistance of the Allies in April, 1918. In September and October, 1918, the enemy troops finally evacuated the country under pressure of the victorious Allied offensive

BRITISH SENTINEL ON NIGHT-DUTY IN FRONT OF THE RUINED CLOTH HALL

THE GERMAN OFFENSIVE OF 1914

(October 29-November 15, 1914.)

Preliminary Operations

After the victory of the Marne, which drove the Germans north of the Aisne, began the operations known as " the Race to the Sea." Each side endeavoured to outpace the other, with the object of surrounding the enemy's marching wing.

This remarkable " Race to the Sea "—a widely extended movement splendidly carried out by General Foch, and in which the Allied forces in their march towards the north constantly outstripped the enemy—might have been used as the starting-point for a grand Allied offensive against the German right, but the exhaustion of the Belgian army, after the terrible trials which it had just gone through in its retreat on the Yser—following on the fall of Antwerp—and the delays in the transport of the British troops from the Aisne front to the north, prevented the development of this offensive.

It was therefore only possible for the Allied armies to fix their front and make it impregnable.

The stages of this race to the sea and the fixation of the front took place between September 20 and October 23, 1914.

The Forces Engaged (Oct. 1914)

When the First Battle of Ypres opened, the front described a wide semi-circle passing through Zonnebeke, Gheluvelt and Zandvoorde, running

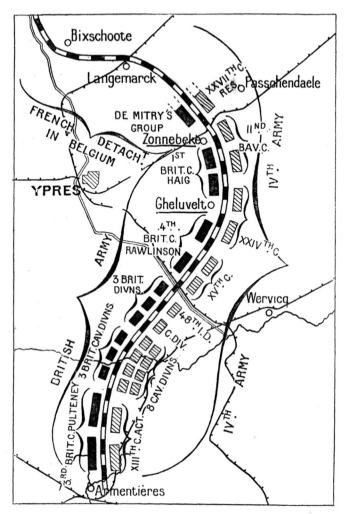

thence south of Messines, and finally linking up with the line to the east of Armentières.

· At the beginning of the battle all this part of the front was held by the British army, as follows: from Zonnebeke to Zandvoorde, the 1st Corps (Haig) and 4th Corps (Rawlinson); from Zandvoorde to Messines, the Calvary Corps (Allenby), two infantry divisions, and the Lahore Division, which had just landed at Marseilles; lastly, from Messines to Armentières, the 3rd Corps (Pulteney).

Facing these forces were the German IVth army, consisting of the XIIIth, XVth and XVIth active corps, and the IInd Bavarian Corps, reinforced during the battle by a Division of the Guards. The British Cavalry Corps had to face four German Cavalry Corps.

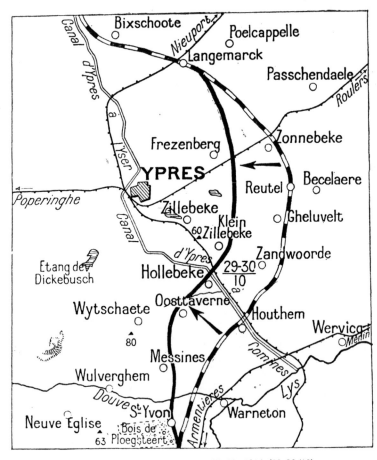

THE GERMAN THRUST OF OCT. 29-30, 1914 (29–30/10)

To make up for their setback in the race to the sea, the German High Command decided on a strenuous effort to break through the Allies' front at Ypres. The "Battle for Calais" was about to begin. The enemy confidently expected to reach the coast, from which they hoped to expose England to such peril as would break down the pride of that troublesome enemy.

The German attack began on October 29 under the eye of the Kaiser, who, for the following five days, took up his quarters at Thielt, whence he arranged to make a triumphal entry into Ypres.

For seventeen days (October 29–November 15) the German regiments, elated by the presence of their Emperor, fought with unheard-of frenzy and an utter disregard of losses in their frantic attacks against the Ypres salient.

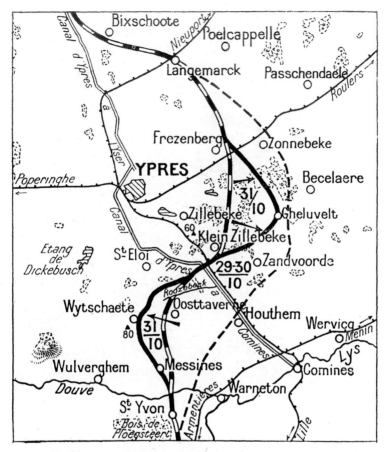

ON OCT. 31, THE GERMANS MADE PROGRESS, SOUTH OF YPRES, BUT WERE
DRIVEN BACK, EASTWARDS, TO GHELUVELT

To the east of Ypres the action fought between Poelcappelle and Gheluvelt
failed. The fierce German attacks, in spite of the masses of men engaged,
broke down before the stubborn resistance of the Allies.

In a counter-offensive the British, supported on their left by French
divisions, reached the village of Becelaere, between Zonnebeke and Gheluvelt,
but were unable to hold it.

Further south, the British were forced to abandon Zandvoorde and
Hollebeke. Gheluvelt, first lost on October 30, was recaptured on the 31st
in a counter-attack by the 1st Corps. Supported by three French battalions,
the British subsequently repulsed all attacks and successfully barred the
road from Menin to Ypres. On the evening of the 31st, the line in the eastern
sector ran as follows : east of Frezenberg, Gheluvelt, east of Klein Zillebeke
and the bend in the canal to the north-east of Hollebeke.

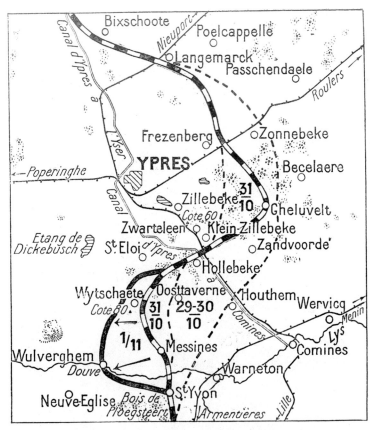

ON NOV. 1, THE SITUATION WAS CRITICAL IN THE EXTREME. THE GERMANS
CAPTURED THE MESSINES-WYTSCHAETE RIDGE, AND THE BRITISH FELL
BACK ON WULVERGHEM

The Germans were more successful to the south-east. After an intense
bombardment they attacked, on October 30, from Saint-Yves to Wytschaete,
capturing Saint-Yves and obtaining a footing in Messines, from which, however, they were immediately driven by a counter-attack.

On October 31, the Germans, after concentrating enormous masses of
troops between Oosttaverne and Roozebeek Canal, made a fresh attack.
In the morning they gained a footing in the eastern outskirts of Messines, but
could get no further, thanks to a counter-attack by three French battalions
with twelve guns from St. Eloi.

The Germans, however, redoubled their efforts, and towards noon, after
a fierce struggle in the streets of Messines, the British cavalry were gradually
forced back, but clung desperately to the western outskirts of the village.
At about 3 p.m. a fierce struggle began for the recapture of the convent to

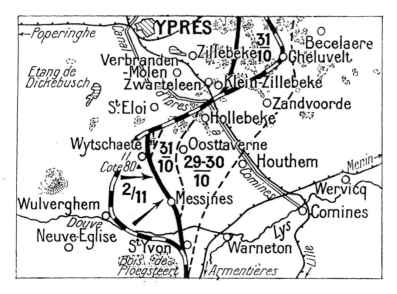

ON NOV. 2, THE FRENCH COUNTER-ATTACKED AND RETOOK THE MESSINES-WYTSCHAETE RIDGE. THE GERMANS LAUNCHED A MASS ATTACK AGAINST GHELUVELT

the south of Messines, then in the enemy's hands. By night the British were in possession of the last houses west of Messines, the Germans holding the eastern crest.

During the night of October 31, the Messines-Wytschaete crest was again fiercely attacked. The Germans gained a footing in Wytschaete and broke the British line to the north of Messines. A withdrawal became necessary, and at dawn the line was set back as far as the western outskirts of Wulverghem.

During the day of November 1, Wytschaete was retaken and lost again.

French Zouaves, acting as reinforcements, held their ground doggedly in front of St. Eloi. The enemy offensive redoubled in intensity, and the situation became desperate. As a result of the flooding of the Yser, the German IIIrd Corps in the northern sector became available and joined in the assault.

The French 14th Corps, hurriedly called up, counter-attacked furiously and succeeded in driving back the Germans and gaining a fresh footing in the western outskirts of Wytschaete. On November 2, the French were once more in possession of the western crest of Messines-Wytschaete.

This check did not daunt the Germans, who, having just been reinforced from their Belgian garrisons, directed their efforts further to the north. The attack was made by compact masses of troops on the St. Eloi-Zwarteleen front, the movement coinciding with a thrust against Gheluvelt on the Menin-Ypres Road. At the latter point the front was momentarily broken,

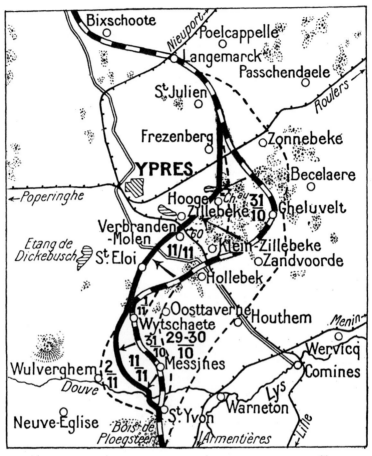

THE GERMANS CONTINUED THEIR FURIOUS ATTACKS UNTIL NOV. 11, BUT
FAILED TO REACH THEIR OBJECTIVE: YPRES

but furious counter-attacks re-established the original positions. The
French troops which held the bend of the canal north-east of Hollebeke were
overpowered and thrown back on Verbranden-Molen. A counter-attack
by the 1st British Corps checked the enemy onrush, and after a magnificent
defence the original line was almost entirely maintained.

The battle continued to rage with increasing violence, the culminating
point being reached on November 11. At dawn the Germans, after a terrific
artillery preparation lasting several hours, attacked with the infantry of
the Ist and IVth Brigades of the Prussian Guards. They succeeded in piercing
the line in three places, and forced their way into the woods behind the
trenches to a depth of rather more than two miles through the principal
breach.

They did not, however, reach their objective. Enfiladed by machine-gun fire, they were partly driven back into their trenches, after a bloody hand-to-hand struggle amid great confusion. The losses on both sides were very heavy, without any decisive result being attained.

The weather, previously bad, now became a violent storm. During the night, under cover of the hurricane, the Prussian Guard broke through the Allies' front. Ypres—the prize on which the Kaiser had set his heart—seemed at last within the enemy's grasp.

But the British, momentarily demoralized, quickly rallied and drove back the Prussians in a heroic charge.

The struggle continued fiercely during the following days, the Germans launching numerous attacks with compact masses of troops. The deep lines of infantry, led by young officers, whose undeniable courage did not compensate for their lack of experience, were mown down.

Exasperated by this check, the enemy set about to destroy the town which they were unable to take. On November 10, German aeroplanes dropped incendiary bombs, and thenceforth the bombardment was conducted methodically both by aeroplanes and by guns firing from ten to twenty shells per minute.

Up to the 13th, the town had suffered comparatively little. The Cloth Hall had only been hit by two shells (on the 5th) and by a few bombs. But in the disastrous days of October 22, 23 and afterwards, the bombardment became more intense and better regulated. The Germans brought up an armoured train to Houthem, which, directed by observation balloons, rained incendiary and explosive shells on the town. On the evening of the 23rd, all that remained of the Place des Halles was a heap of ruins.

THE CLOTH HALL IN FLAMES (NOV. 22, 1914)
The Germans, unable to capture Ypres, destroyed it methodically by shell-fire
(photo, Antony, Ypres).

DURING THE WINTER MONTHS LOG-ROADS WERE NECESSARY FOR THE LORRIES
AND ARTILLERY, AND EVEN THESE SANK IN THE BOTTOMLESS MUD

Period of Comparative Calm

(December, 1914–April, 1915.)

Having failed to pierce the front in the neighbourhood of Ypres, the Germans abandoned their attacks in close formation, and operations in this sector were soon limited to incessant artillery actions, occasionally followed by fierce surprise attacks at isolated points.

Some of the attacks during this period of comparative calm are worthy of note.

On December 10, the Germans launched three attacks against the British troops in front of St. Eloi, only one of which gave any result. The enemy captured the first trenches of the Allies' line, but were driven out on the following night by a counter-attack.

Other attempts were made during the following week, with the same negative result.

On December 17, the Germans attacked in force to the north-west of Ypres. Zonnebeke, Langemarck and Bixschoote were bitterly disputed, and the two last-named villages remained in the hands of the enemy.

These battles were fought in a sea of mud formed by the rain and the flooding of the land by the Belgians.

One Colonel wrote: "The ground on which we are fighting is awful. There is a crust about a foot thick which is comparatively good, but underneath there is bottomless mud. Men standing in trenches four or five feet deep are almost unable to get out, and gradually sink until it takes several men to extricate them."

The first fortnight of January was comparatively quiet. During the second fortnight a strong German attack broke down before the front-line trenches near Bixschoote.

The continual rains in this previously flooded district rendered all activity

THE FRONT-LINE DURING THE WINTER CAMPAIGN OF 1914–1915

impossible, save that of the artillery, which continued to bombard unceasingly during February.

It was only in the first half of March that the opposing armies became really active. From the 5th to 11th, powerful German attacks were repulsed between Dixmude and the Lys.

The British, on their part, were not inactive during this period. They fought a vigorous action between the Lys and La Bassée, captured Neuve-Chapelle after prolonged strenuous fighting, and took a thousand prisoners, including several officers.

As the weather conditions improved, the number of local engagements increased. In an enemy attack on St. Eloi, between March 12 and 18, the British first lost and then recaptured that village. Further south, during the first half of April, fierce engagements were fought without decisive result in front of the villages of Kemmel and Wulverghem.

The Germans continued to bombard Ypres with large calibre shells, heaping ruins upon ruins.

THE SECOND BATTLE OF YPRES

(April—May—June, 1915.)

The long period of enforced inaction during the winter months, and the depressing waiting in the icy mud, were now succeeded first by local enemy attacks, then by a fresh powerfully organised attempt by the Germans to capture Ypres.

The battle began on April 14 with a strong unsuccessful thrust to the north of Ypres. The British replied by attacking Hill 60.

On April 17, after the firing of a powerful mine, the hill was brilliantly captured, and in spite of bitter counter-attacks on the 18th by the Germans, who fully realised the importance of this *point d'appui*, the position remained in the hands of the British.

Meanwhile, a new German offensive was being prepared, which their High Command believed would prove irresistible, thanks to the use of a new weapon, as murderous as it was unexpected.

Although Germany had signed the clause of the Hague Convention (July 29, 1899), which prohibits the use of **asphyxiating gas**, the unscrupulous leaders now made use for the first time of this treacherous weapon.

In accordance with their usual practice, they claimed that the British used the gas first, and that they used it only in reprisal. Needless to say, this assertion was pure fiction.

On April 22 the front ran as follows : Belgian troops held the canal ; the French 45th Colonial Infantry Division, resting on the canal, and passing through Bixschoote, linked up with the troops of the Canadian 3rd Brigade.

Throughout the morning of April 22, the Germans bombarded the first lines, while the roads behind were swept by the fire of the heavy artillery, including 16½-in. guns. The bombardment continued into the afternoon.

Suddenly, at about 4 p.m., there rose from the German trenches, opposite the lines occupied by the French Colonial troops, a strange opaque cloud of greenish-yellow fumes. A light breeze from the north-east wafted this cloud towards the French, who, a few moments later, fell gasping for breath in terrible agony. Terror spread through the ranks, especially among the African troops. A panic inevitably followed, which quickly spread from the front to the rear lines.

Behind that cloud of gas the German troops advanced, protected by a heavy barrage and intense machine-gun fire.

The French Colonial troops fell back several miles towards Ypres, and the Germans took Steenstraat, Het Sas and Pilkem, together with many prisoners.

The withdrawal of the French uncovered the left flank of the Canadians, who were on their right, and they in turn were obliged to fall back, leaving four guns in the hands of the Germans.

In the afternoon the Canadians, rallying, took the offensive, recovered

THE FIRST GERMAN POISON-GÁS ATTACK
(*April* 24, 1915.)

part of the lost ground between Steenstraat and Langemarck, together with their guns, and inflicted a sanguinary defeat on the Germans.

Further north, on the Yser Canal, the enemy took advantage of the disorder caused by the gas to cross at Steenstraat Bridge, and reached the village of Lizerne near Zuydschoote, where they strongly entrenched themselves. But Zouaves, aided by Belgians, counter-attacked in force, retook Lizerne, and advanced along the canal.

The greatest German effort was made on April 25 against the British lines.

The attacking troops had been grouped on both sides of the railway from Ypres to Roulers, near Broodseinde, but in spite of fierce attacks they could not break the British lines, and once more their dastardly methods failed them.

At the end of April the front was fixed as follows : from Steenstraat the line followed the canal as far as Het Sas Bridgehead and then passed along the right bank to Pilkem (on the opposite bank). Here it turned at right-angles eastwards, as far as Soetart Farm (on the Ypres-Langemarck Road), turned south-east through Wieltje, then west of Hooge, finally linking up with Hill 60 and St. Eloi.

The Germans revenged themselves for their failure by again bombarding Ypres.

The shelling, which had ceased for a time prior to the offensive, began again with renewed intensity. An enormous quantity of heavy artillery had been brought up, and large calibre shells were continuously rained on the unhappy city, causing a panic. The few remaining inhabitants fled terror-stricken along the Poperinghe Road.

During the last week of April the battle continued with great bitterness, but in spite of the enemy's use of gas, the Allies gradually retook the lost ground. Then followed a fresh period of calm, broken from time to time by fierce attacks, of which that of May 5 on Hill 60 was the most important.

On May 8 the battle broke out afresh in the region lying between Poelcappelle and the Ypres-Menin Road. The Germans pierced the British line at several points, notably between St. Julien and Frezenberg, and reached Wieltje, but after bitter hand-to-hand fighting, they were driven back to their trenches at the point of the bayonet.

The next day the attack was renewed in close formation, under the protection of an intense bombardment of gas shells, but the British, now provided with masks, stood firm. The German columns, mown down by shrapnel and machine-gun fire, were unable to reach the British trenches.

The fighting died down during the next few days, on account of rain and wind storms, which made all movement impossible, but began again on the 24th without, however, any appreciable advantage for the Germans, who once more took the offensive.

Another period of calm set in, and this Second Battle of Ypres—the second serious check of the Germans before the town—ended in a successful operation by the British, who, on June 2, captured the Château of Hooge on the Menin Road, two miles from Ypres.

Long period of comparative calm. Isolated actions. Artillery activity on both sides

(June, 1915–June, 1917.)

These weeks of fierce, bloody fighting were followed by a long period of comparative calm, the operations having been transferred to other parts of the front (Argonne, Artois, Champagne). Nevertheless, local actions took place from time to time without any appreciable result. From July 22 to 26 the British, after successful mining operations, advanced their line along the Ypres-Menin Road, in the neighbourhood of Hooge Château.

After being driven from the outskirts of the château by a gas attack on August 7, they retook the lost ground on the 8th and advanced beyond it.

Towards the middle of September there was a rather severe bombardment near Steenstraat and Ramscappelle, while Ypres received 300 more shells.

During the latter half of August an Order of the Day to the German Armies in Flanders stated: " *Our work is practically finished in the East, and we are on the point of beginning in the West ; peace in October is certain.*"

THE FRONT LINE FROM JUNE 1915 TO JUNE 1917

In December, a new offensive by the Germans failed, despite the use of gas. There was unusual artillery activity, all the heavy guns, both German and British, being brought into action.

On December 30, Field-Marshal French received the title of " Viscount of Ypres," in commemoration of the vigorous British defence of that city.

On February 12, 1916, the Germans launched fresh attacks in the west, near Steenstraat and Het Sas, and attempted to cross the Yser. After being smartly checked, they furiously attacked the British trenches between the Ypres-Comines Canal and the railway, and succeeded in capturing one of them for a length of 600 yards. This trench, on account of its frequently changing hands, came to be known as the " International Trench." A few days later (March 2) the British retook it.

The struggle now became limited to a continuous artillery duel, with occasional surprise infantry attacks. The hamlet of St. Eloi to the south was the scene of constant fighting for the possession of the shell-craters.

On April 19, the fighting assumed a more serious character. An unimportant German attack near St. Eloi and along the Ypres-Langemarck Road was the prelude to operations by considerable enemy forces, having for their objective the great undulating slopes between Hill 60 and Armentières.

BRITISH DEFENCE WORKS IN FRONT OF YPRES

The first of these attacks took place on April 25, 1916, but failed. Two days later a night attack with gas was repulsed with hand grenades.

A third attempt was made in May, 1916, more to the south towards Armentières, on the sides of the road connecting that town with Ypres. The British, entrenched in a wood near Ploegsteert Village, were assailed by three German columns, and were only able to repulse two of them. The third took the position, but Scottish troops counter-attacked and drove the Germans back.

The most important of the enemy attacks during this period took place on June 1. The preparations included a concentration of troops between Tournai and Baisieux, from May 21 to 27, supported by guns of all calibres.

The attack was carried out in considerable strength between Hooge and the Ypres-Comines Railway.

The artillery preparation began at 9.15 a.m on June 1, and at noon the first assaulting wave entered the front-line trenches. The battle died down for a few minutes in the evening, only to break out again during the night. The Germans succeeded in crushing in the front to a depth of some 700 yards in the direction of Zillebeke, but the next day a portion of the lost ground was retaken by the Canadians.

On June 6, a fresh assault began, preceded by the usual bombardment, and further assisted by mine explosions. The front line trenches to the north of Hooge were lost; but on the 13th the valiant Canadians, who had

THE FLANDERS BATTLEFIELD IN WINTER

previously recaptured the original positions abandoned on June 1, resumed the offensive, and re-established the lines from the southern part of Sanctuary Wood to a point 1,000 yards north of Hill 60.

Throughout the days of June 26 and 28 there was an extremely violent bombardment, to which the British guns replied effectively. The Germans, whose losses from the attacks and this artillery fire were very heavy, declared : " *Belgium will be our grave.*"

These were the last operations in which the enemy took the offensive. All their efforts had failed, whether their object had been to turn the left flank of the Allies, to break the lines around Ypres, or merely to take the town.

THE ALLIED OFFENSIVE OF 1917

Series of powerful attacks with limited objectives. From June to October, the stages of the offensive were punctuated by breathing spaces, during which the conquered ground was consolidated, in view of counter-attacks, and the artillery brought up, to prepare the following attack.

Preliminary Operations

The Capture of Messines Ridge by the British

(June 7, 1917.)

From July, 1916, to May, 1917, the Ypres sector remained comparatively quiet. There were few attacks on either side, but the guns thundered day and night. It may be said that the British were " trying their hand."

In June, 1917, certain at last of their strength, they made their first big effort, and step by step, in accordance with a carefully worked-out plan, they completely liberated Ypres by a series of offensives lasting four months, and broke the iron circle which, for two years, had been strangling the town.

For several months before the battle, the attack on Messines Ridge had been carefully planned by means of a model in relief, situated in the open air and covering an area about equal to that of a tennis court. Here were reproduced in relief all the contours and peculiarities of the ground. Everything, down to an isolated tree trunk, was reproduced.

British effort took definite shape for the first time on June 7. The attack, planned by Sir Douglas Haig, had for its objective the capture of the crests between Wytschaete and Messines, which the Germans had seized on November 1, 1914.

For seven days an artillery preparation of incredible intensity hammered the villages of Messines and Wytschaete, until they had completely disappeared.

On June 7, about an hour before dawn, at 3.10 a.m., the sky was lit up by an intense light, while a series of terrific explosions were heard ; nineteen mines, some of whose galleries had taken more than a year to bore, exploded along the enemy positions.

The Germans were taken completely by surprise, and gave way before the impetuous onrush. In a few minutes their first line was carried along the whole of the attacked front. Then, almost without a pause, the British troops attacked the western slopes of the Messines-Wytschaete Ridge, and by about 6.30 a.m. held the crests along the whole line.

The village of Messines offered resistance, but was captured by the New Zealanders in a vigorous attack, as was also the village of Wytschaete. By noon the second stage of the offensive was about to begin.

Descending the eastern slopes of the ridge the British carried a second strong position, then attacked a fresh line—chiefly in Rayon Wood—in which were large shelters of reinforced concrete, each capable of holding a company. At about 4 p.m. Oosttaverne Village, lying west of the centre of the position, fell. At sun-down the day's objectives had been completely attained, and the advance at certain points exceeded two miles in depth.

This fine success was due to the carefully detailed preparation carried out under the orders of General Herbert Plumer, to the destructive effect of the mines, to the violence and precision of the bombardment, to the excellent co-operation of the Air Forces, and to the harmonious working together of all arms. The tanks rendered excellent service.

THE BRITISH OFFENSIVE OF JUNE 7, 1917, AGAINST MESSINES RIDGE,
PRECEDED BY THE FIRING OF NINETEEN ENORMOUS MINES

The Germans made an effort to rally, but their first counter-attacks, near Oosttaverne and to the east of Messines, failed.

At about 7 p.m., on June 8, a fresh German counter-attack was launched along the whole of the new front between St. Yvon and the Ypres-Comines Canal. Other engagements were fought to the east of Messines and near Klein Zillebeke. Although reinforced by fresh divisions, the German attack was broken by midnight.

Resuming their offensive, the British, on the morning of June 11, captured the whole system of German trenches, nearly a mile in length, situated near Poterie Farm, to the south-east of Messines. The next day fresh progress was made along nearly two miles of the front to the north-east of Messines, and the hamlet of Gapaard occupied.

THE FRONT LINE BEFORE THE ALLIES' OFFENSIVE OF JULY 31, 1917

After the offensive—limited in scope—of June 7, which reduced the salient, south of Ypres, the British continued to press the enemy. Frequent raids kept the Germans on the alert and secured important *points d'appui*.

On June 14, the Germans were forced to abandon an important part of their first-line trenches between the Lys and St. Yvon. On the same day a considerable advance was made east of Ploegsteert Wood, and in the immediate neighbourhood of Gapaard Village.

During the night of the 14th a double attack was made : one to the east of Messines ; the other along both banks of the Ypres-Comines Canal, to the north-west of Hollebeke. These attacks gave the British a large number of trenches, which they held in spite of fierce counter-attacks.

To sum up, during the latter half of June an advance of 500 to 1,000 yards in depth was made along the whole front line between Klein Zillebeke and the Lys.

The month of July passed in raids, patrols, and reconnoitring, preparatory to the new offensive of July 31.

This far-reaching offensive, which lasted from July 31 to the end of October, may be divided into six successive phases, and ended with the liberation of Ypres.

First Phase

(*July* 31—*August* 15.)

Capture of the First and Second German Lines

When the battle began, the firing line extended from Dixmude, along the Yser Canal, then followed the Yperlée River, on the left bank of the Yser Canal. It next passed through Lizerne to Het Sas, whence it followed the canal to Boesinghe. Opposite this village the line crossed the canal and the Ypres-Bruges railway, then passed the Quatre-Chemins cross-roads, descending thence to Essenfarm and Kruppfarm, which lie on either side of the Pilkem Road. Continuing west of Wieltje Village, it passed south of Verlorenhoek Château, skirted Verlorenhoek Village, and descended west of Hooge, after crossing the Ypres-Roulers railway. It next skirted the northern part of Sanctuaire Wood, then entered the latter, coming out to the south of Zwateleen. From there, the line extended southwards, passing west of Hollebeke, east of Gapaard, and skirting the eastern fringe of Ploegsteert Wood.

During the fortnight preceding the offensive, changes were made in the order of the forces holding the line.

British troops relieved the Belgians and French who had been operating near the coast, in the direction of Lombaertzyde. Moreover, the French forces, placed at the disposal of General Anthoine, had taken up positions between the Belgians and the British from Reninghe to Elverdinghe.

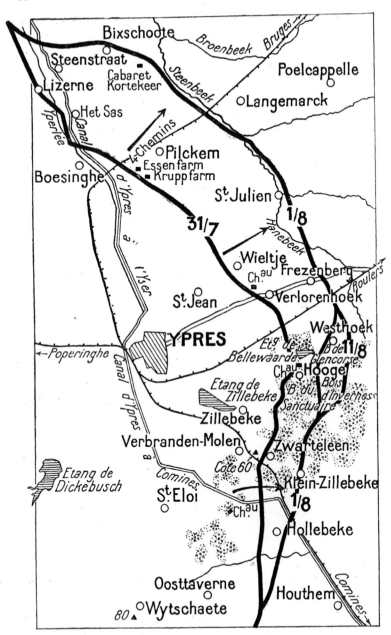

FIRST STAGE OF THE ALLIES' ADVANCE FROM JULY 31 TO AUGUST 11, 1917
(31/7–11/8)

At 4 a.m. on July 31, in spite of unfavourable weather, the British troops, under the command of Generals Plumer and Gough, co-operating with the Franco-Belgian troops led by General Anthoine, attacked in force along a front of fourteen miles from Dixmude to the Lys.

In the French sector, the greater part of the troops had crossed the Yser during the night. The artillery then pounded the first and second German lines, and as soon as the range had been lengthened, the infantry dashed forward. At the scheduled hour the first and second enemy lines from Dixmude to Bixschoote, to a depth in places of almost two miles, were occupied, while Bixschoote, Steenstraat, and Kortekeert Inn fell.

The British were on the right of the French. The Ypres-Roulers Road formed the axis on which their attack turned. On the left of this road they pierced the German lines to a depth of nearly two miles, and occupied the bridges over the Steenbeek Canal. Several villages were captured : Verlorenhoek, Frezenberg, St. Julien, Pilkem, in addition to a large number of fortified farms and woods.

On the right of the Ypers-Roulers Road, the British encountered a very strong resistance. The ground, more broken than that on the other part of the battle-front, and also intersected with woods, enabled the Germans to keep several *points d'appui*. Despite the fiercest fighting, it was impossible to drive them out of part of the second position on the right wing. Nevertheless, an advance of about a mile in depth was made in this sector, and the village of Hooge and Sanctuary Wood were captured.

On their extreme right the British had captured Hollebeke Village early that morning.

The next day (August 1), the Germans replied but feebly in the French sector, while in the British sector, in spite of the rain, they counter-attacked with the greatest fury.

Near St. Julien the line fell back slightly, but along the rest of the front the positions were fully maintained.

The first phase in the liberation of Ypres was over.

In forty-eight hours, the offensive, methodically prepared and carried out, had attained the objectives, given the Allies more than 6,000 prisoners and an immense quantity of stores.

During the following days, in spite of torrential rain, the Germans attempted unsuccessfully to retake the lost ground, some of the attacks being particularly fierce.

In the sector held by the French troops there was little more than a heavy bombardment on either side. French raids on fortified farms held by the Germans resulted in slight progress being made to the north of Bixschoote and Kortekeer Inn.

The British, on the other hand, had to face strong counter-attacks. On August 1, the Germans succeeded in regaining a footing in their old advanced positions along the Ypres-Roulers Road. On the 2nd, the British lines between St. Julien and the Ypres-Bruges railway were attacked in force. The village of St. Julien was lost, but was finally retaken on the 3rd. On the 4th, the British line was advanced beyond St. Julien.

On August 5, during a fresh attack on both banks of the Ypres-Comines Canal, the Germans retook Hollebeke, but were driven out almost immediately.

On the night of the 5th they again attacked Hollebeke, but without success.

On the 10th, an interesting operation was carried out by the British. The front attacked was shorter than in the offensive of July 31, and extended about a mile and a half to the south of the Ypres-Roulers Road.

Early in the morning the British were in complete possession of Westhoek Village, after which a violent struggle took place for the high ground round the village. By evening all the objectives had been attained, including the capture of Westhoek Crest and Glencorse Wood.

August 12 was marked by six enemy counter-attacks, which caused a slight withdrawal of the line to the south of Glencorse Wood. Everywhere else the Allies' positions were fully maintained.

Second Phase

(August 15–September 19, 1917.)

The Allies resumed their offensive on August 15 along a front of some nine miles, from the Yser Canal to the Ypres-Menin Road.

The attack began at 4.45 a.m. The French attacked on both sides of the Steenstraat-Dixmude Road, crossing the Steenbeek stream in the morning. Driegrachten Bridgehead was taken after hand-to-hand fighting, while in the evening the whole of the strip of ground between the Yser and the Martjet-Vaart Canal was in the hands of the French.

The British operating on the right of the French rapidly attained their first objectives, then vigorously following up this first success, they took by asault the village of Langemarck and its strong defences, advanced 800 yards beyond the village and captured the whole system of trenches.

To the south, along the Ypres-Menin Road, the struggle was more stubborn, the Germans resisting desperately. A series of furious counter-attacks enabled them finally to preserve their line practically intact in this district.

The day's captures included more than 2,000 prisoners, of whom thirty were officers, and twenty-four guns, including several of large calibre.

Desperate fighting continued until September 19 without, however, altering the positions established on August 15.

On August 19, the British, by small local attacks, advanced about 500 yards on the Ypres-Poelcappelle Road and captured several fortified farms.

The Germans made desperate efforts to hold the high wooded ground comprising Polygone and Inverness Woods, near the Ypres-Roulers Road.

On the 22nd the fighting increased in fierceness. The British advanced only with great difficulty, and the eastern edges of Inverness Wood were hotly contested.

In these combats, from which neither side gained any decisive advantage, the Germans made use for the first time of liquid fire, thanks to which innovation they succeeded temporarily in retaking the north-western corner of Inverness Wood, but were soon driven out.

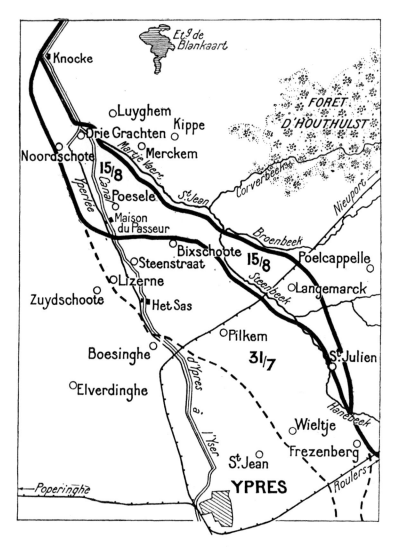

SECOND STAGE : THE ATTACK OF AUGUST 15 (15/8)

Further north, the British, on August 24 and 25, advanced their lines to the north of St. Julien and Langemarck.

During the following days, persistent rains prevented any further operations. Infantry actions were now succeeded by continuous bombardments on both sides, and by isolated raids.

Third Phase

(*September* 20–*October* 3, 1917.)

On September 20 a fresh offensive was begun along the whole front from Langemarck to the Ypres-Menin Road, a distance of eight miles.

The part assigned for the French troops under General Anthoine was merely to protect the left wing of the British Army which, pivoting on Hollebeke, was to wheel and advance its marching wing in a direction at right-angles to the Zonnebeke-Gheluvelt line.

All the objectives were attained at an early hour.

Inverness Wood, which had been hotly disputed for the six previous weeks, was taken by the London troops.

The Australians retook by assault Glencorse Wood — lost a few days before—and Nonnes Wood. The Scottish and South African Brigades captured the fortified farms of Vampire and Borry, and the Potsdam and Anzac Redoubts. Lancashire Territorials carried Iberian Farm and next day (the 21st) Gallipoli Farm.

The British then attacked the second German lines. On the right the Territorials* fought violent engagements to the north of the bend in the Ypres-Comines Canal, near Klein Zillebeke, and in the vicinity of the position known as Tower Hamlet.

In the centre, progress was more important. The ground hereabouts rises in a small plateau about 220 feet in height, which dominates the whole battlefield and extends in two long spurs : one running north-east towards Zonnebeke, the other southwards towards Menin. The Germans had fortified these positions very strongly and withdrawn their main line of defence to the eastern edge of the plateau, *i.e.* opposite the side by which the enemy must attack. This line protected the village of Zevenkote and the western edge of Polygone Wood, leaving in front the woods of Nonnes, Glencorse and Inverness, and Herenthage Park, the eastern edge of which latter it followed. The woods were strongly fortified, and the British had twice previously (July 31 and August 16) vainly endeavoured to capture them.

It was the Northern troops and the Australians who carried these positions, advancing to a depth of 1,700 yards and taking Veldhoek and the western part of Polygone Wood—the principal centre of the German resistance. Further north, Zevenkote was captured and the London Territorials, supported by the Highlanders, seized a second line of farms.

In the evening of September 20, the front ran approximately as follows : from Rose Farm (700 yards west of Poelcappelle) to Fokker Farm (on the eastern edges of Zevenkote) ; across the western part of Polygone Wood—including Veldhoek—then to the east of Herenthage Château, and ending at Hollebeke.

The Germans, in their costly and unsuccessful efforts to retake the lost positions, suffered exceedingly heavy losses, without gaining any advantage.

On the morning of the 26th the British continued their attack along a five-mile front, from the east of St. Julien to Tower Hamlet near the Ypres-Menin Road.

The rest of Tower Hamlet Spur was captured, in addition to the whole of Polygone Wood.

Further north, a fresh advance of 1,700 yards was made, and the strongly fortified village of Zonnebeke remained in the hands of the British.

Besides the gain in ground, more than 4,000 prisoners were taken.

The Germans, by a series of powerful counter-attacks, sought to win back

---

* French : troupes des comtés = county regiments.

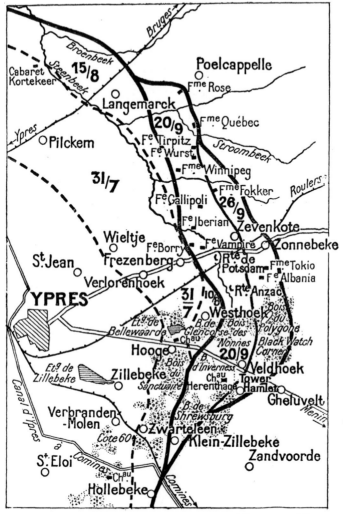

THIRD STAGE: BRITISH ADVANCE FROM SEPT. 20 TO SEPT. 26
(20/9–26/9)

the lost positions. On the evening of the 26th, four attacks were made in the neighbourhood of Tower Hamlet.

On the 27th they attacked the village of Zonnebeke, while on the morning of the 30th three attacks were made, without result, on both sides of the Ypres-Menin Road.

On October 1 the Germans attacked three times on a front of 1,700 yards to the south of the Ypres-Menin Road, while the same night two fresh assaults gave no appreciable result.

BATTERY OF BRITISH HEAVY HOWITZERS IN ACTION

Fourth Phase
(*October* 4–8, 1917.)

The increasing activity of the Germans did not in any way prevent the British from preparing a fresh offensive.   On the morning of October 4, English divisions, supported by Welsh, Scottish and Irish battalions, attacked along a front of ten miles, between Tower Hamlet and the north of Langemarck. The Germans, disconcerted and surprised by this unexpected attack—they were themselves preparing to attack with five divisions—fell back from the beginning of the action.

A rapid advance of one-half to nearly two miles was made.

South of the Menin Road the objectives were attained almost at the outset.

To the north of the same road the enemy resistance was more stubborn. Nevertheless, the villages of Reutel and Polderhoek, together with the château of that name, were captured, freeing at the same time the top of the crest, whose eastern slopes run down to the village of Bacelaere. Further north, the Australians captured Noordhemhoek and Molenaarelsthoek, reached Broodseinde Crest, and thus advanced beyond the Bacelaere - Broodseinde Road.

On the other side of the Ypres - Roulers railway, the British drew appreciably nearer Passchendaele, captured

PART OF THE GROUND COVERED BY THE OFFENSIVE, SEEN FROM AN AEROPLANE

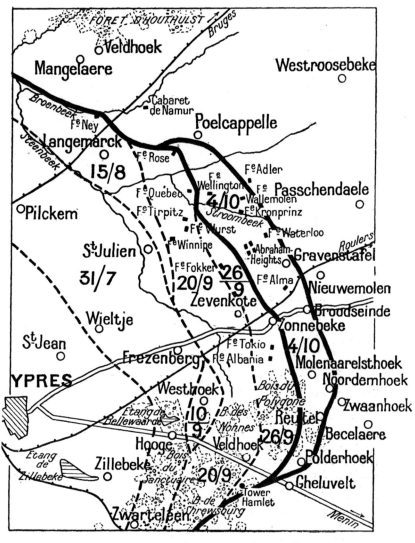

FOURTH STAGE : THE 4TH OCTOBER, 1917 (4/10)

Gravenstafel and a certain number of fortified farms, and approached the western outskirts of Poelcappelle.

In spite of the violent storm which was then raging, all the objectives were attained and the line of crests conquered.

Owing to the very large numbers of troops massed on the front at the time of the attack, the German losses, which included 4,500 prisoners, were particularly heavy.

A DIFFICULT CROSSING. BRITISH AND BELGIAN SOLDIERS

Fifth Phase

(*October* 9–12, 1917.)

To completely clear Ypres, a few strongly fortified villages beyond the line of crests captured on October 4 had still to be taken. These formed the objective of the attacks of October 9 and 12.

On October 9, in spite of the appalling weather, the British attacked again on a front stretching from St. Janshoek (a mile north of Bixschoote) to the south-east of Broodseinde. The French were holding a front rather less than two miles in length to the north of Bixschoote, and had for objective the southern edge of Houthulst Forest.

The signal to attack was given at 5.30 a.m. Despite the rain, which had been falling incessantly for several days, the infantry crossed first the canal in flood, then a veritable sea of mud, and captured Mangelaere and Veldhoek. They advanced rather more than a mile and reached the south-western edge of Houlthulst Forest, after having captured numerous strongly fortified farms and blockhouses.

The British sector extended from the north-west of Poelcappelle to Broodseinde, and formed a front of some seven miles.

On the right, the Manchester Regiment and the Lancashire Fusiliers advanced from 1,600 to 2,000 yards in the direction of Passchendaele, and carried the line beyond the crests occupied on October 4.

In the centre, many farms, redoubts and blockhouses were captured.

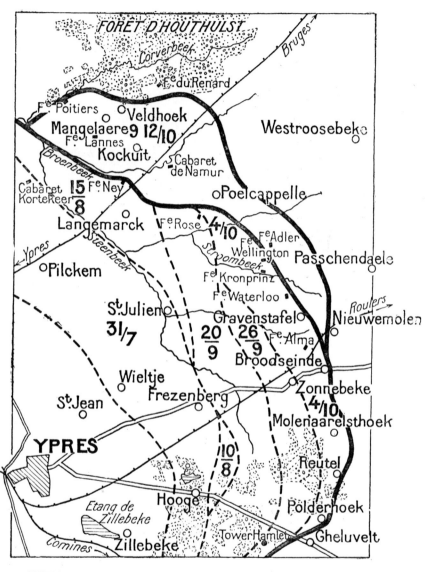

FIFTH STAGE: THE BRITISH ATTACK HOUTHULST FOREST AND APPROACH
PASSCHENDAELE

To the north, the capture of Poelcappelle was completed, the British joining hands with the French on the outskirts of Houthulst Forest.

More than 2,000 prisoners were taken.

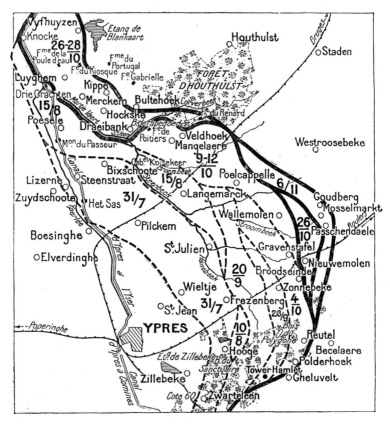

SIXTH STAGE: BY NOV. 6, YPRES WAS COMPLETELY CLEARED

Sixth Phase

(October 22–November 6, 1917.)

After a short rest, during which the new positions were consolidated—in view of enemy counter-attacks—the battle broke out afresh on October 22.

The attack of the 22nd was, in reality, only of secondary importance, but thanks to the progress made, it was possible to carry out the operations of the 26th on a larger scale than originally intended.

In order definitely to consolidate the captured positions, it was still necessary to take the village of Passchendaele, which stands on the high ground dominating the plain of Flanders to the east of Ypres and from which Roulers is visible.

A fresh offensive was accordingly begun at dawn on October 26.

In the French sector, the troops, after wading through the St. Janshoek and the Corverbeek streams with the water up to their shoulders, stormed the village of Draeibank, Papegoed Wood, and many fortified farms.

The next day fresh progress, to a depth of more than a mile, was made on both sides of the Ypres-Dixmude Road, along a front of two and a half miles. The villages of Hoekske, Aschhoop, Merckem, and Kippe were captured, and the western edges of Houthulst Forest reached.

On the 28th, the advance continued on the left, in co-operation with the Belgians. The French took the village of Luyghem, and the Belgians Vyfhuyzen.

The British, on their part, advanced in the direction of Passchendaele, as far as the southern slopes of the village, capturing a whole series of positions east of Poelcappelle.

On October 30, British and Canadians continued their attacks, and in spite of the enemy's desperate resistance, reached the first houses of Passchendaele.

FRENCH TROOPS PASSING IN FRONT OF THE RUINS OF YPRES CLOTH HALL

On the following days they improved their positions. The struggle at this juncture was very bitter, Hindenburg having shortly before issued an order stating : " *Passchendaele must be held at all costs, and retaken if lost.*"

On the morning of November 6, the British resumed the offensive. The Canadians, after bloody engagements to the north and north-west of Passchendaele, captured the hamlets of Mosselmarkt and Goudberg, and finally carried Passchendaele.

On the evening of November 6, Ypres was completely cleared ; and from the top of the Passchendaele Hills the valiant British troops could see, stretching away to the horizon, the Plain of Flanders, which had been hidden from the Allies since October, 1914.

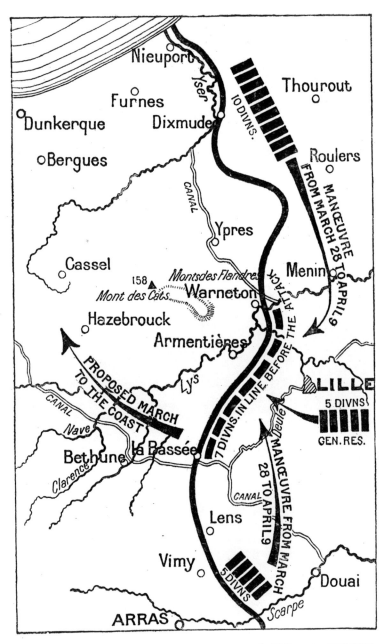

PREPARATION OF THE GERMAN OFFENSIVE OF APRIL 9, 1918. THE OBJECTIVE

SCHERPENBERG HILL

The German Offensive of 1918

The front was quiet during the winter of 1917–1918, but 1918 opened darkly for the Allies.

The Treaty of Brest-Litowsk had sealed the defection of Russia, while Roumania, reduced to her own resources, was forced to sign the Treaty of Bukarest. Lastly, invaded Italy was only just recovering from the disaster at Caporetto. Already, in spite of the terms of the Brest-Litowsk Treaty, huge masses of troops, guns and stores were being despatched to the Western Front. The blow fell on March 21, 1918.

The objectives, three in number, were the smashing of the British right wing at its junction with the French ; the separation of the two Allied army groups ; the driving back of the Channel coast of the two British armies, after they had been surrounded on the south. The long-coveted road " *Nach Paris* " would then at last be open.

But in spite of their colossal efforts the Germans were held.

By March 31, the German Imperial forces were exhausted, and General Foch was able to say : " *The wave has spent itself on the beach.*" The peril seemed to be averted.

But the respite was only a short one. The German attack before Amiens was scarcely stayed (April 6) when the battle suddenly broke out again. From the Arras sector to La Bassée the whole line was ablaze as far as the Lys. While, in the first German offensive the British right had suffered severely, it was against the left wing of the same army that the new blow was struck.

The new offensive, although quickly prepared, was even more violent than the first.

On April 9, when the attack began, the German battle-front between the Lys and La Bassée was held by twenty-one divisions in line and six in reserve, under the command of Von Quast (VIth Army).

Of these twenty-seven divisions only seven were in line on March 28.

Ten divisions were hurriedly brought up from the Belgian front (IVth Army—Von Arnim), which was holding the sector from the Lys to the Channel. Five others were despatched from the Artois front, and, lastly, five divisions were taken from General Ludendorff's general reserve.

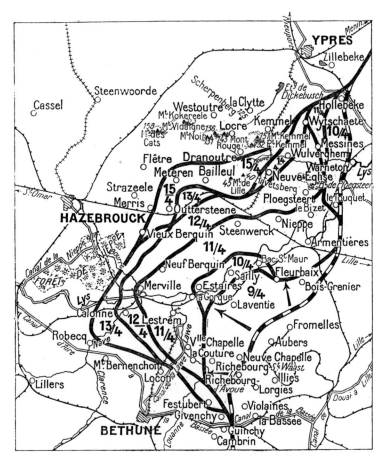

ON APRIL 9-20, 1918, THE GERMANS BROKE THROUGH THE ALLIES' FRONT, SOUTH
OF YPRES, AND ADVANCED TO NIEPPE FOREST AND THE CHAIN OF THE
FLANDERS HILLS

THE BATTLE OF THE FLANDERS HILLS

The Break-Through

April 9, 1918.

The Germans began the attack on the morning of April 9, after an intense
bombardment with gas shells, and under cover of a dense fog reached the
first machine-guns. The sector was held by Portuguese troops, wedged in
between the British, from Bois-Grenier to Neuve-Chapelle.

On the whole length of front attacked, between La Bassée and Armentières, in the Plain of Flanders, the only natural obstacles are the rivers and

canals. From the beginning of the battle the Portuguese were thrown into disorder by the extreme violence of the attack.

The twenty-one German shock divisions attacked in five columns : to the south, the first column in the direction of Givenchy ; the second (General Kraevel), in front of Festubert ; the third (Von Bernhardi) marched against La Couture and Richebourg-St.-Waast ; the Carlowitz Corps, forming the fourth column, advanced against Estaires in the direction of Laventie ; further north, the fifth column attacked in the direction of Fleurbaix, outflanking Bois Grenier and Armentières on the west.

Under the pressure of the attack, a depression was formed in the line. Fleurbaix, Laventie, Richebourg-St.-Waast and Neuve-Chapelle were lost, and the Germans reached the Lys between Estaires and the St. Maur Ferry. To the north of the pocket the Allies resisted successfully at Fleurbaix ; to the south, Givenchy, after a desperate struggle, remained in the hands of the British.

On the following day the German troops, continuing the push towards the centre, succeeded in crossing the Lys between Estaires and the St. Maur Ferry.

The battle extended northwards and the IVth Army (Von Arnim) attacked between Armentières and Ploegsteert with the Eberhardt, Marschall and Sieger Corps.

The push continued on the 11th, and Armentières, outflanked on the north and south, smashed by the shells and drenched with gas, had to be evacuated.

On their left, the Germans, after crossing the Lawe, north of Locon, two miles from Béthune, captured Neuf-Berquin and Merville.

Givenchy, held by the British 55th Division, resisted all attacks and remained in their hands.

On the right, Nieppe and Steenwerk had to be evacuated. The German advance to the south of Armentières becoming more pronounced, the British straightened their front, to avoid too sharp a salient, and fell back to the Messines-Wytschaete Crest.

On the 12th the fighting continued furiously. Advancing along the Lille-Hazebrouck railway, the Germans reached the outskirts of Nieppe Forest. South-west of Merville they captured Calonne, and, further north, approached Bailleul.

North of the Lys, under pressure of Von Arnim's army, the Messines-Wytschaete Crest, with the wood and village of Ploegsteert, had to be abandoned. The British line was withdrawn to Neuve-Eglise and Wulverghem. In these few days the gains of the Allied offensive of the last five months of 1917 were lost.

The 13th marked the culminating point of the battle in the central sector. Foch made his dispositions promptly, and French reinforcements were despatched to the critical points.

Von Bernhardi crossed the Clarence at Robecq on the 13th. On the same day Von Gallwitz made a strong push northwards between Hazebrouck and Bailleul, with the object of outflanking the line of the Flanders Hills, already attacked on the east and north-east by the IVth Army (Von Arnim).

Battles were fought south of Meteren, at Merris, Vieux-Berquin and on the eastern outskirts of Nieppe Forest. To the east of Bailleul, Neuve-Eglise (an important cross-road) was fiercely disputed. After changing hands many times on the 14th, it was finally abandoned the same night.

The loss of Neuve-Eglise led to that of Wulverghem, and the British were forced to fall back to the eastern slopes of Kemmel Hill, the first high point in the chain of hills called the Heights or Hills of Flanders. From east to west this chain consists of Rouge Hill (flanked on the north-east by Scherpenberg), Vidaigne Hill, Noir Hill, Cats Hill, and lastly by the western bastion of Cassel.

After taking Neuve-Eglise on the night of the 14th, the Germans decided on a fresh and still more powerful effort.

Three picked divisions were hurled against the hills of Lille and Ravetsberg, to the east of Bailleul, which fell. The Germans entered Bailleul, pushing on thence to Meteren, which they also captured. The next day they tried to develop this success, but instead of the exhausted British, the Germans now found themselves faced by fresh French troops. In three days (April 12-14) Pétain had brought up without a hitch five French divisions and one cavalry corps, which stayed the German rush at the foot of the hills.

ROUGE HILL, SEEN FROM SCHERPENBERG HILL

On April 16 the Germans made their first attempt to turn the Flanders Hills from the south-west in the direction of Hazebrouck.

The French 133rd Infantry Division (Valentin), supported by the British 34th Division, vigorously repulsed the attack.

On the 17th a fresh and more powerful attack was made simultaneously from the north-east, towards Poperinghe, and from the south, on the Bailleul-Neuve-Eglise front.

At the same time an independent operation—which failed completely—was undertaken to the north of Ypres on the Belgian front. The Belgians repulsed the Germans and took 800 prisoners.

To the south three British divisions (34th, 49th, 19th) stayed the German advance.

A last effort, starting from Wytschaete, also broke down before the French 28th Infantry Division (Madelin).

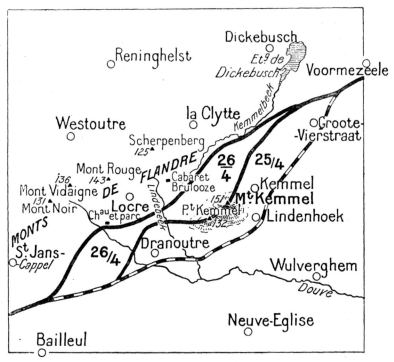

THE GERMANS ATTACK THE CHAIN OF HILLS WHICH PROTECT YPRES

The Capture of Kemmel Hill

(*April* 22–28, 1918.)

A period of comparative calm followed, during which the Germans prepared a fresh mass attack, in view of the capture of the Hills.

For this new offensive five fresh divisions from Alsace-Lorraine were brought up, of which two—the IVth Bavarians and the Alpine Corps—were picked troops. These troops joined the four divisions already in the sector. The artillery was also considerably reinforced.

During this concentration small local attacks occurred on both sides.

On April 22 and 23 the Germans endeavoured to improve their positions north of Bailleul, but without appreciable result.

The French, on their part, sought by attacks and raids to impede the preparations for the coming assault.

At that time the firing line, from west to east, ran as follows: from Meteren (held by the Germans) it passed north of Bailleul, then crossed the crest of Lindenhoek at Dranoutre, east of Kemmel, and skirted Groote Vierstraat and St. Eloi on the east.

The five French divisions which defended the Hills occupied the following positions :

The 133rd before Cats Hill ; the 34th Infantry (Sabatier) before Locre ; the 154th Infantry (Breton) from Dranoutre to the Petit-Kemmel ; the 28th Infantry (Madelin) before Kemmel Hill, its left linking up at Linden-hoek with the British 9th Infantry Division. The Cavalry Corps was held in reserve on the Hills.

At 2.30 a.m. on April 25 the attack began with a heavy bombardment, in which the proportion of gas shells was far greater than previously.

At about 6 a.m. the infantry assault began in a dense fog north and south of Kemmel Hill.

North of the Hills the " Sieger " divisions, marching west to east, had orders to capture Kemmel Village, and then, *via* the Valley of the Kemmel-beek, join up at Locre with the Eberhardt Divisions, which were attacking from north to south in the direction of Dranoutre.

On the left of the attacking front, the village of Kemmel was taken by the Germans, in spite of a heroic defence. Step by step the British 9th Division was driven back into Kemmelbeek valley and on Dickebusch Pond.

In the centre the enemy storm-troop waves, after several repulses, finally reached the summit of Kemmel Hill, where a fierce hand-to-hand encounter took place. In spite of their great heroism, the 30th Infantry Regiment, outnumbered and almost surrounded, was forced to abandon the position, but only after a dashing counter-attack by a battalion of the 99th Infantry had failed to extricate them. On the right, the German Alpine Corps, by a daring manœuvre, made possible by the fog and the broken nature of the ground, succeeded in reaching the artillery positions, which were at once attacked by machine-gun fire. The French and British batteries, under a storm of bullets, were obliged to retreat, saving what material they could and blowing up the rest.

The Germans thus reached the village of Locre, which changed hands several times during the day.

Finally, after a counter-attack, the 154th Infantry Division remained masters of the village, although the Germans succeeded in holding the " hospice " at the southern end.

The situation was now critical and the enemy advance had to be checked at all costs. On the night of the 25th the Allies were reinforced by the 39th Infantry Division (Massenet) at the very moment a fresh German offensive was being launched. The timely arrival of these troops effectually stayed the German thrust.

On the evening of the 26th, after much sanguinary fighting, the enemy paused, exhausted. The French took advantage of the respite to consolidate new positions.

The 27th was marked only by a violent attack on the extreme left at Voormezele, where the Germans succeeded in obtaining a footing, only to be driven out by a vigorous British counter-attack.

As a result of these various battles the new line was as follows : from Locre Château it ran south of Locre Village, followed Kemmelbeek Valley, passed in front of La Clytte Village, then south of Dickebusch Pond and Voormezele Village, joining up with Zillebeke on the south-east.

It was against this new front that the Germans were now preparing a new offensive.

THE LAST GERMAN ATTACK

(*April* 29, 1918.)

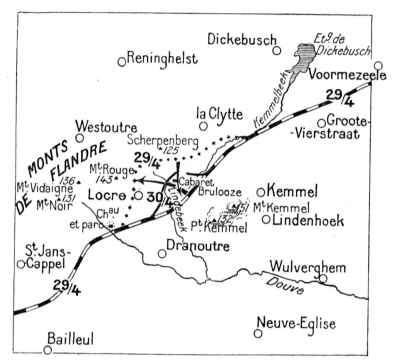

ON APRIL 29, THE GERMANS LAUNCHED A LAST FURIOUS ATTACK AGAINST THE HILLS, AND FAILED. EXHAUSTED, THEY THEN ABANDONED THEIR PLANS FOR TAKING YPRES

After an artillery preparation lasting all night, the attack began at 7 a.m. on April 29, along a front about eight and a half miles in length, extending from the Château and Park of Locre to Dickebusch Pond. This attack, by no less than 120,000 enemy troops, resulted in a crushing defeat for the Germans.

Both ends of the front stood firm : the British on the left, between La Clytte and Zillebeke, and the French on the right, in the Château and Park of Locre. All attacks were vigorously repulsed, and the Germans did not even reach the Allied lines.

More fortunate in the centre, they succeeded in taking the village of Locre, and advanced beyond it as far as the cross-ways on the Westoutre Road, half-a-mile north of Locre. Their success was but short-lived, however, as a vigorous counter-attack by French Dragoons drove them back, and at the end of the day all that remained of their gains was a slight salient near Brulooze Inn. Exhausted, they did not renew their attack.

The Hill offensive was over. The Germans had destroyed Ypres, but could not enter the ruined city.

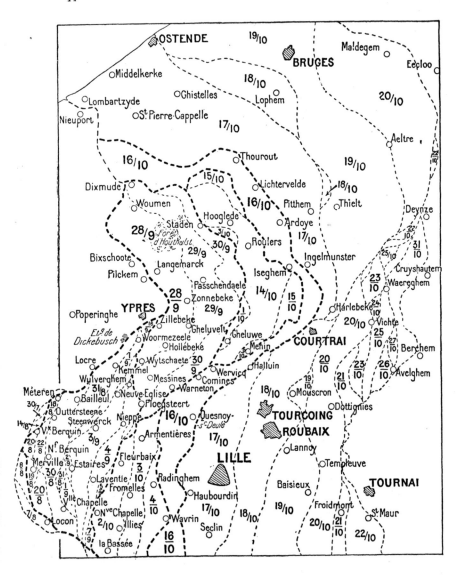

THE ALLIES' VICTORY OFFENSIVE OF AUGUST-OCTOBER, 1918

After the German setback of April 29, the initiative passed into the hands of the Allies.

On April 30, the French 39th Infantry Division reduced the Brulooze Inn salient. During the following week numerous local engagements enabled the Allies to recapture several fortified farms and *points d'appui*, and generally to consolidate their positions. An attack by the British, on July 19, to the north of the Lys, advanced their lines two and a half miles, and gave them the village of Meteren. Then followed a lull, which lasted until the speeding-up of Foch's offensive rendered the German positions untenable and forced the conquered enemy back towards the Rhine.

After the Allies' victorious counter-thrust had flattened out the " pocket " made by the German Spring offensive near Amiens, the battle quickly spread over the whole front, including Flanders.

East of Nieppe Forest and Hazebrouck, the British, pressing forward towards Armentières, advanced beyond Vieux-Berquin in the direction of Merville. On August 18, they joined battle between Vieux-Berquin and Bailleul, on a front of four miles, and captured the village of Outtersteene. The next day they entered Merville.

GERMAN POSITION NORTH OF YPRES, CAPTURED BY BELGIAN TROOPS
ON SEPT. 8-9, 1918

On September 1, the British had reached the line : La Bassée, Laventie, Steenwerke, Neuve-Eglise and Wulverghem, on both sides of the Lys. On the following day, Estaires was outflanked south of Lens, and the famous Hindenburg line passed. Noreuil, Villers-au-Flos (south of Quéant), Le Transloy, Sailly-Saillisel and Allaines (south of the Bapaume-Cambrai Road) were next captured. Further south the storming of Quéant by the Canadians, who then advanced beyond, and approached Marquion, opened the road to Cambrai.

On September 4, the British reached the Canal du Nord, and crossed it at several points. On the following day, they regained possession of their old lines on both sides of the Lys, from Neuve-Chapelle to Givenchy, and captured Ploegsteert Village. On September 10, south-west of Cambrai, Gouzeaucourt Wood and the old line of trenches dominating Gouzeaucourt Village, as well as the outskirts of Havrincourt Wood were occupied.

The general offensive was to be launched a few days later, in co-operation with the Belgian Army and some French units.

On September 28, the Belgian Army and the British Second Army (General Plumer), commanded by King Albert, marched against the army of Von Arnim. The British, covered on the north by the Belgians, began a turning movement in the region of Lille, Roubaix and Tourcoing. Houthulst Forest, the crests of Passchendaele and Gheluvelt, and Dixmude were carried with fine dash. Crossing the Lys on the following days between Wervicq and Comines, the British now drew near to Menin. On October 1, the Germans were in full retreat on a wide front north and south of the Bassée Canal, all their positions between Armentières and the south of Lens being now abandoned.

DESTROYED BRITISH TANK SUNK IN THE MUD AT THE ENTRANCE TO
POELCAPPELLE

On October 9, the Canadians of the First Army occupied Cambrai. On the 13th, the British reached the gates of Douai and occupied the banks of the Haute-Deule Canal from Douai to Vendin-le-Vieil.

Elsewhere, the British Second Army, after capturing Menin and Wervicq, obtained a footing on the right bank of the Lys, then crossed the river between Menin and Armentières, thus forcing the Germans to abandon the line of the Haute-Deule, and taking the Lille-Tourcoing in the rear.

The British army and some French units occupied Lille—capital of the north—on October 17, and the same days the Germans evacuated Douai. Roubaix and Tourcoing were liberated the next day, and Denain, Marchiennes and Orchies on the 21st and 22nd.

The Western suburbs of Valenciennes were fiercely disputed, being finally retaken on November 2 by the Canadian troops under General Currie.

A few days later the Armistice was signed, and the victory of the Allied armies sealed.

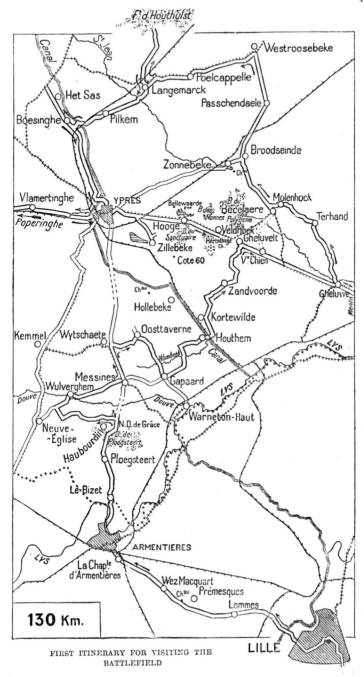

FIRST ITINERARY FOR VISITING THE
BATTLEFIELD

GERMAN OCCUPATION OF LILLE. TROOPS PARADING IN THE GREAT SQUARE
From the Michelin Guide: " Lille, before and during the War."

VISIT TO THE BATTLEFIELD

A visit to Ypres Town and Salient requires two days, and may be made most conveniently by taking Lille as the starting-point.

First Day : Visit Messines, Wytschaete, Houthem, Zondvoorde, Gheluvelt, Becelaere, Zonnebeke, Passchendaele, Langemarck, Ypres, Zollebeke and Hooge, spending the night at Poperinghe.

Second Day : Visit the Hills: Scherpenberg, Vidaigne, Rouge and Kemmel ; then, after re-crossing the French frontier, those of Cats and Noir, returning to Lille for the night, *via* Armentières, Estaires, Béthune and La Bassée.

FIRST DAY: LILLE—YPRES

(See Itinerary, p. 47.)

Starting-point : The Grande Place, Lille.

Take Rue Nationale to the end, go round Place Tourcoing, take Rue de La Bassée on the left, then the first turning on the right (Rue de Turenne), Canteleu Gate, and Rue Lequeux. Cross the bridge over the Haute-Deule Canal, and turn to the left into N. 42.

At Canteleu follow the tram-lines leading to Lomme. At the end of the village, cross the railway (l. c.). Go through Lomme by Rue Thiers, leaving the church on the right (transept greatly damaged).

On the left are the burnt ruins of a large spinning mill. In the fields : numerous small forts of reinforced concrete, which commanded all the roads into Lille. The road passes through a small wood, in the right-hand part of which are the ruins of Premesques Château, of which only the façade remains. Further on, to the left, is Wez Macquart, whose church was badly damaged. Trenches lead to the road, while in the fields, traces of the violent shelling are still visible.

Pass through Chapelle d'Armentières (completely destroyed). After crossing the railway (l. c.), a British cemetery is seen on the right. **Armentières** *lies on the other side of the next level crossing.*

After entering **Armentières,** *and immediately beyond the railway, take Rue du Faubourg de Lille, leaving the Church of St. Roch on the right. After passing a public washing-place, turn to the right into the Rue de Lille, then cross the Grande Place.* Here will be seen the Hôtel-de-Ville, completely ruined. *Take a few steps along Rue de Dunkerque, then turn into the first street on the right, which leads to the Place de l'Eglise St. Waast.*

Armentières

Armentières suffered in many wars, being taken by the English in 1339, by the French in 1382, by the Calvinists in 1566, by Marshals de Gassion and De Rantzau in 1645, and by the Archduke Leopold in 1647.

ARMENTIÈRES *(ancient engraving)*

Occupied by the Germans in August, 1914, it was retaken in September. Nearly four years later (April, 1918) it again fell into the hands of the enemy. On October 2, it was finally liberated by General Plumer's army.

Until the later war, Armentières had preserved its 17th century belfry of chimes, its church of Nôtre-Dame, and another church dedicated to St. Waast—patron saint of the town.

This personage, to whom many of the churches in this district have been dedicated, was Bishop of Arras in the 6th century. While still a priest, he is said to have cured a blind beggar in the presence of Clovis. This miracle was one of the causes which led to the conversion of the king, to whom St. Waast acted instructor in the Faith.

The town also possessed a national technical school, dating from the previous century.

VIEW OF ARMENTIÈRES (*before the War*)
THE RIVER LYS AND ST. WAAST CHURCH (*Cliché LL.*)

Belfry, churches, schools and houses are all in ruins.

In everything connected with the spinning and weaving of linen Armentières, like Lille, Roubaix, Tourcoing, and the whole of Northern France in general, was considerably in advance of Germany. Consequently, the Germans destroyed all the mills, factories and metallurgical works, and what machinery could not be taken to pieces and sent to Germany they ruthlessly smashed.

ARMENTIÉRES. ST. WAAST CHURCH AS THE GERMANS LEFT IT
(*Compare with photo, p. 50.*)

ARMENTIÉRES AND THE RIVER LYS

ARMENTIÈRES. THE HÔTEL-DE-VILLE AFTER THE FIRST BOMBARDMENT

ARMENTIÈRES. BEFORE RETREATING, THE GERMANS MINED THE TOWN

ARMENTIÈRES. NÔTRE-DAME CHURCH WAS NOT GREATLY
DAMAGED BY THE BOMBARDMENTS (*see below*)

Visit the ruins of **St. Waast Church,** *then return to Rue de Dunkerque.
There take the first street on the right and cross the Lys.* From the Bridge
there is a general view of the church.

ARMENTIÈRES. NÔTRE-DAME CHURCH, WHICH THE GERMANS BLEW UP
BEFORE BEING DRIVEN OUT OF THE TOWN (*see above*)

ARMENTIÈRES. RUE NATIONALE, AS THE SHELLS LEFT IT

ARMENTIÈRES. RUE DE LILLE IN RUINS

BIZET. POST ON THE FRONTIER
On the left of motor-car : TEMPORARY CUSTOM HOUSE

Cross the Cloth Market, then follow the tram-lines along Rue de Flandre and Rue Bizet. Follow the Lys Canal, then cross the new bridge. Go through Bizet Village (badly damaged houses). *Leaving the ruins of the church on the right, turn first to the right, then to the left* (the photograph shows an army hut on the left, now temporarily used as the office of the Receiver of French Customs). *Cross the frontier a few yards further on, then at the fork just outside the village, take the road on the right opposite the Villa des Roses (photo below). Leaving on the right the road to the gasworks* (of which nothing is left but a wrecked gasometer) *the first houses of* **Ploegsteert** *are reached.* This village lay west of the first lines in May, 1918, and was captured by the Germans on April 12 (see p. 39).

BIZET. END OF VILLAGE, GOING TOWARDS PLOEGSTEERT
Take the right-hand road.

BRITISH CEMETERY AT THE ENTRANCE TO PLOEGSTEERT

MESSINES ROAD (*seen from the Château de la Hutte*)
In the background : MESSINES RIDGE

BRITISH CEMETERY ON THE PLOEGSTEERT ROAD AT MESSINES

British cemetery No. 53 (photo, p. 56) lies at the entrance to the village. *Go straight through the village* (in ruins). *On leaving it,* Cemetery No. 54 is seen on the right, then beyond a large concrete shelter, Cemetery No. 55. Cemetery No. 56 is on the left, beyond the level-crossing.

Cross Ploegsteert Wood, leaving the road to Petit-Pont Farm on the left. Here the road rises. To the left, on the slopes of Hill 63, are seen the

CROSS-ROADS AT NÔTRE-DAME-DE-GRÂCE

The Messines Road (bordered with tree stumps) was not practicable for motors in June, 1919. Take the Neuve-Eglise Road on the left (see Itinerary, p. 47).

AMONG THE RUINS OF MESSINES

The motor takes the left-hand road to Wytschaete (see p. 47).

ruins of La Hutte Château. On the crest opposite stand the ruins of Messines (photo above). In June, 1919, it was not possible to go direct to Messines, the road being cut at the Petite Douve stream.

Follow the road as far as the fork to the place called Nôtre-Dame-de-Grâce (the ruins of the chapel are barely distinguishable), *then take the Neuve-Eglise road on the left.* Stop the car at Rossignol terre-plein and walk a few yards into the little wood on the right ; numerous concrete shelters, from the top of which there is a very fine view over the Hills Kemmel, Rouge, Noir and Cats. The last-named can be recognised by its abbey, which stands out against the sky.

Return to the car. The road now descends. Passing by a few ruined houses—all that remain of the hamlet of Haubourdin—a fork is reached, where take the Neuve-Eglise-Messines road on the right. British cemetery on the right. *Cross the Douve river, then the railway (l. c.). Turn to the right at the first ruins of Wulverghem, then go through the village, passing in front of the cemetery. Next cross the Steenbeck, by the St. Quentin Bridge. The road now rises sharply to the crest on which Messines used to stand.* Numerous small forts are seen to the right and left. These machine-gun nests are all that now mark the site of the village.

At the entrance to the village leave the car at the junction of the Ypres-Armentières and Neuve-Eglise-Warneton roads, and visit these pathetic ruins on foot.

Messines may be regarded as one of the hinges of the " Ypres Salient." An important strategic point, it was hotly disputed throughout the war.

ENTRANCE TO WYTSCHAETE
The motor takes the right-hand road to Oosttaverne (see p. 47).

On November 3, 1914, during the First Battle of Ypres, it fell into the hands of the enemy. At four o'clock on the following day, the ground between this village and Hollebeke (some four miles to the north) was the scene of several furious attacks (see p. 8).

Messines was destroyed by the British bombardment during the offensive of June, 1917. The New Zealanders captured it on June 7, in spite of a stubborn defence. They also took the neighbouring village of Wytschaete (see p. 20). Messines again fell into German hands in April, 1918 (see p. 39), and was finally retaken on September 30 during the last battle (see p. 46).

Return to the car and take the Ypres road on the left (photo, p. 58). Along this road are numerous little bridges thrown across the shell-holes.

Wytschaete, which is soon reached, was captured, like Messines, in the first battle of 1914, and retaken by the New Zealanders on June 7, 1917. After being entirely destroyed by bombardment (see p. 20), it was lost again on April 15, 1918, then retaken on September 30, 1918.

At the fork, just before entering the village—protected by a series of powerful blockhouses—*take the road on the right leading to Oosttaverne* (now totally destroyed). *Follow the main road* (Ypres-Warneton) *on the right as far as the place called Gapaard* (photo below), *then turn to the left along the road to Houthem.* A series of little bridges over shell-craters full of water—once the River Wanbecke—are crossed.

GAPAARD. END OF VILLAGE, GOING TOWARDS HOUTHEM

HOLLEBEKE CHÂTEAU, BEFORE THE WAR. IT HAS BEEN
RAZED TO THE GROUND (*photo, Antony, Ypres*)

Go through Houthem, which was razed to the ground. Beyond an armoured shelter built against the brick wall of a house, *the road turns to the left. Cross the canal by the temporary bridge.*

The old bed of the canal is marked by some crumbling blocks of concrete. *A few yards further on, take the level-crossing over the Ypres-Lille Railway.* It was on this line that on October 22 and 23, 1914, the Germans brought up an armoured train which bombarded Ypres with incendiary shells, causing the first serious damage to the town.

A few hundred yards beyond the railway turn to the right at the village of Kortewilde, where a few wooden houses are being erected among the ruins. *After crossing a number of little bridges over the Gaverbeck canal, the road, rising slightly, turns to the right.* At this turning the Château (photo above) and village of **Hollebeke** ought to be visible on the left, but this part of the battlefield is in so chaotic a condition that neither road, canal, nor village can be distinguished.

WHERE GHELUVELT USED TO STAND, ON THE ROAD TO MENIN

During the first battle (November, 1914) the Germans launched attacks in great force between Hollebeke and Messines, and captured both these places. Hollebeke was retaken on July 13, 1917, during the first phase of the great British offensive for the clearing of the town. After being lost again in April, 1918, Hollebeke was finally recaptured by the Allies in October.

The road first rises, then descends. On the hillside are the ruins of Zand-voorde. *At the entrance to the village take the Zillebeke Wervicq road on the left, then first to the right, then to the left, between two wooden houses. The road descends, then, undulating slightly, joins the main road from Ypres to Menin, opposite Gheluvelt,* the site of which is marked by a sign-post.

This was one of the important strategic points in the first German offensive of 1914 (see p. 7), when the village was captured by the enemy. During the battle for the clearing of Ypres, fierce fighting took place to the west of **Gheluvelt,** especially at Tower Hamlet. From November, 1917, to April, 1918, the firing-line ran through the village. Gheluvelt was retaken by the British in October, 1918.

Take the main road from Ypres to Menin on the right. Only at Gheluvelt will a passable road to Becelaere be found.

In Gheluvelt, where there are still a few broken walls standing, turn to the left at the fork in the road, leaving the ruined church on the right. At the next fork take the right-hand road to the ruined hamlet of Terhand.

Fifty yards before the crossing with the Dadizelle Road, there is a German cemetery on the right, containing a remarkable concrete monument, thirty feet in height, which dominates the whole plain. This monument (photo, p. 62)

ROAD FROM GHELUVELT TO BECELAERE
(*Impracticable for motors in June,* 1919.)

GERMAN CEMETERY AT TERHAND. DUMMY FUNERAL MONUMENT WHICH WAŚ
REALLY A GERMAN OBSERVATION-POST

was in reality a German observation post. Inside there were two floors.
An outside staircase led to a platform. Traces of the balustrade are visible
in the photo.

Leave the Dadizelle road on the right. The road hereabouts is camouflaged. Numerous small forts may be seen on both sides of the plateau,
especially on the right. The largest of them was used as a telephone exchange.

After passing the place called Molenhoek the tourist comes to the
Passchendaele-Wervicq road, now impassable.

*Leave the car at the fork, and go on foot through the ruins of Becelaere,
as far as the church on the right.*

RUINED VILLAGE OF BECELAERE

Return to the fork and take the right-hand uphill road. On the plateau there are many shelters.

To the west of the road from Becelaere to Zonnebeke lay Polygone Wood, which was entirely destroyed. The British made two unsuccessful attempts (July 31 and August 16, 1917) to take this strongly fortified wood, succeeding eventually on September 20 (see p. 28). Evacuated by the British in April, 1918, the wood was finally recaptured by the Allies in October, 1918.

Beyond the place called Noordenhoek there is a bend in the road. On the left, Zonnebeke Pond, the ruined château, and the remains of a gasometer come into sight (photo below).

At the place called Broodseinde take the Ypres-Roulers road on the left, to visit the ruins of Zonnebeke.

Zonnebeke was taken in 1914 by the Germans, who made an outpost of it in front of their lines. The village was recaptured on September 26, then lost in April, 1918, and finally retaken in the following October.

Return to the fork (which was commanded by numerous small forts), *and turn to the left:* military cemetery at the side of the road. In the fields on the right, 200 yards beyond the level crossing, there is a monument to the memory of 148 officers and men of the Canadian 85th Battalion (photo, p. 64).

Passing through shell-torn country, **Passchendaele**—now razed to the ground—is reached. All that remains of the church is the mound seen in the background of the photograph (p. 64).

Passchendaele was captured by the Germans in November, 1914, and later by the British (October 26, 1917). The village had already been wiped

RUINS OF ZONNEBEKE VILLAGE

BETWEEN BROODSEINDE AND PASSCHENDAELE. MONUMENT TO 148 FALLEN
OFFICERS AND SOLDIERS OF THE 85TH CANADIAN BATTALION

out by the bombardment, but the position, which dominated Ypres and
Roulers, was an important one. The fighting there was of the fiercest,
Hindenburg having ordered it to be held at all costs. However, the British
broke down the enemy's stubborn resistance.

WHAT WAS ONCE PASSCHENDAELE. THE CHURCH WAS ON THE
HILLOCK IN THE BACKGROUND

WESTROOSEBEKE, SEEN FROM THE RUINED CHURCH

From Passchendaele to Ypres

Beyond the church turn to the left. The undulating road goes straight to **Westroosebeke.**

Westroosebeke was taken at the same time as Passchendaele, during the British offensive of October 29, 1917. These two positions, lost in April, 1918, were retaken on September 30 by the Belgian army under King Albert.

The village was completely destroyed. *On entering, turn to the right and pass the church.* A few broken tombstones mark the site of the churchyard.

POELCAPPELLE. THE ROAD FROM LANGEMARCK TO DIXMUDE

C

Retracing his steps, the tourist turns to the right into the Ypres-Roulers Road, which describes a bend to reach **Poelcappelle.** This village was the scene of fierce fighting in December, 1914, and May, 1915, and is now in ruins. There are numerous redoubts to right and left. *Just beyond the village, leave the Dixmude Road on the right, and take the one leading to Langemarck.*

Beyond the cross-roads there is a confused heap of rails and broken trucks in the middle of a piece of shell-torn ground.

At the fork, take the road to the right and enter the ruined village of **Langemarck.**

The photograph below shows : in the background, a mound formed by the ruins of the church ; in the foreground, a tank.

Langemarck, defended by the French in 1914, was evacuated on December 17 of that year. Recaptured, the town was lost again on April 21, 1915, during the German gas attack.

Keep along the road, leaving on the left the ruins of the church, and a little further on the remains of the château (photo, p. 67).

Cross the railway (l. c.) and then go on to **Houthulst Forest,** captured by the Germans in 1914, and retaken in 1918 (see p. 46). In June, 1919, the roads through the forest were impracticable for motor-cars

Return to the fork at the entrance to Langemarck, turn to the right, and take the road to Boesinghe, crossing the Hanebeek. The road follows the Ypres-Thourout railway, on both sides of which are numerous redoubts. *Cross the ruins of Pilkem,* 300 yards beyond, which is a rather large British cemetery.

At the next fork in the road turn to the right and cross the railway (l. c.). On the left is another cemetery. *Turn again to the left.* Notice in passing a third cemetery, then a few yards further on the ruins of a mill. *Cross the canal at the Pont de Boesinghe.*

On reaching the crossing of the main road from Dixmude to Ypres, turn to the right. On the left, the remains of Boesinghe Château stand in the middle of a park, the trees of which are cut to pieces.

LANGEMARCK, WITH DESTROYED TANK. THE MOUND IN THE MIDDLE DISTANCE IS ALL THAT REMAINS OF THE CHURCH

LANGEMARCK CHÂTEAU BEFORE THE WAR

Now razed to the ground (photo, Antony, Ypres).

Follow the road running along the canal. The latter, owing to the upheaval of the ground by shell-fire, is often lost to view. 1,500 yards from Boesinghe, the site of Het Sas village, where the lock used to stand, may still be located. The fighting was very severe there, especially in 1914.

BOESINGHE, RUINED CHÂTEAU AND DEVASTATED PARK

ENTRANCE TO YPRES. YPRES CANAL AT BOESINGHE, SEEN FROM
RUE DE DIXMUDE, YPRES

(Compare with view below, taken before the War.)

Return to Boesinghe, leave the road just taken on the left, and cross the railway (l. c.).

The road runs alongside the Yperlée river and canal for some distance. Numerous traces of footbridges are to be seen over both river and canal, the course of which can no longer be distinguished with certainty.

The road next turns sharply to the left, crosses the Lys-Yperlée Canal, then passes the dock of the Yser-Ypres Canal (photo above), *and enters* **Ypres** *by the Dixmude Gate.*

ENTRANCE TO YPRES BEFORE THE WAR

(See above—photo, Antony, Ypres.)

GENERAL VIEW OF YPRES, BEFORE THE WAR (*photo, Antony, Ypres*)

YPRES

Few names awaken more memories than that of Ypres—a city of incomparable splendour in the Middle Ages, and of which nothing now remains but a heap of ruins. Of the last precious traces of this ancient prosperity, the rich and splendid buildings which filled the mind with wonder—the immense Cloth Hall, the beautiful cathedral, the churches, the sumptuous mansions, the sculptured houses—the German guns have spared nothing. History furnishes few examples of such grandeur followed by destruction so swift and so complete. Ypres is now but a memory.

Chief Historical Events

The Town of Ypres (Latin Ypra, Flemish Ieperen) grew up in the 10th century around a fortified castle, rebuilt about 958 by Baudoin, Count of Flanders. This castle had been in existence since the 8th century, but only the ruins had survived Norman invasions.

The town, favourably situated in the centre of the maritime plain with its rich grassy meadows intersected by canals, prospered exceedingly. A numerous population sprang up of merchants and artisans, whose chief sources of wealth were the manufacture and sale of cloth.

As early as the 12th, but especially in the 13th and 14th centuries, Ypres, thanks to important privileges granted by the Counts of Flanders, became a considerable town, and possessed 4,000 looms.

Flanders, the meeting-point of the three great European states—England, France and Germany—was then the industrial centre *par excellence* of the west and the rendezvous of all the merchants of the old world. This explains the splendour of the towns of Flanders in the Middle Ages, not only Ypres, but Bruges, Ghent, etc.

This prosperity was often a temptation to the Kings of France, who led many an expedition into Flanders. Ypres was taken by Louis VI. in 1128, by Philippe-Auguste in 1213, by Philippe-le-Bel in 1297, but the town was little damaged in these wars.

It suffered more in the 14th century. Riots, and the siege and destruction of the town by the people of Ghent in 1383, caused many of the weavers to emigrate, and left as its only industry the manufacture of Valenciennes lace. At that time the Counts of Flanders were French princes. Robert de Béthune was succeeded in 1322 by the Count of Nevers, whose family reigned until

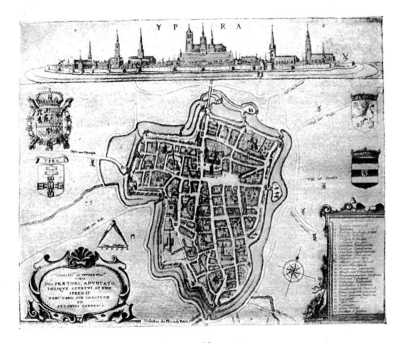

YPRES IN THE 16TH CENTURY

1384. This dynasty ended with Louis-le-Mâle, and Philippe-le-Hardi, Duke of Burgundy, became Count of Flanders. Under the rule of these Dukes, who were fairly wise and moderate statesmen—Flanders being a source of considerable revenue, and the Flemish people quick to revolt against any violation of their privileges—Ypres prospered greatly.

In 1481 Flanders passed under the rule of Austria (Marie, heiress of Burgundy, had married the Archduke Maximilian), then in 1558 under that of Spain. In 1559 it replaced Thérouanne as the centre of the diocese.

At that time it had lost much of its splendour. Towards the end of the

15th century it was depopulated by a dreadful pestilence, and about the middle of the following century, a second outbreak completed the ruin of the town. It was just beginning to recover when it was captured by the *Gueux* and the troops of the Duc d'Albe and Alexandre Farnèse, who massacred most of the inhabitants.

In the 17th century Ypres was taken by the French on four occasions— 1648, 1649, 1658 and 1678—finally reverting to France under the Treaty of Nimègue at about the latter date. Vauban fortified it. Retaken by the Imperial Troops in 1715, Ypres was restored to France in 1792, and under the Empire became the capital of the Département of Lys. The treaties of 1815

GERMAN BOMBARDMENT OF THE ASYLUM

gave it back to the Netherlands, and since 1830 it has formed part of the Kingdom of Belgium.

In 1914 the population numbered 18,000. Its principal industries were the manufacture of woollen goods, printed cottons, linens, ribbons, and Valenciennes lace. Its tanneries and dye works were also of considerable importance. It was a clean, well-built town, watered by the river Yperlée. The many arms of the latter ran through the streets of the town, enabling the boats loaded with merchandise to come right up to the warehouses.

These waterways are now coverd in. Formerly there was a path on each side of them, which explains the exceptional width of the streets and squares of Ypres.

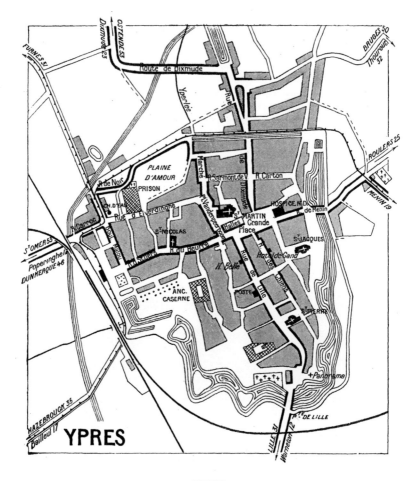

YPRES

A Visit to the Ruins

The tourist enters Ypres by the Dixmude Gate.

At No. 54 Rue de Dixmude is the façade of the Maison Biebuygk, on the right. Built in 1544, this house was one of the most remarkable in Ypres. Immediately below the gable were two carved medallions representing the sun and the moon. The great pointed arch which framed the gable windows gave exceptional grace to the façade (photos, p. 73).

At No. 66 of the same street, on the left, the 18th century façade shown in the photographs (p. 74), was still standing in July, 1919. It was decorated with statues of the Virgin Mary and St. François, under fluted niches with carved borders.

BIEBUYGK HOUSE (*No. 54, Rue de Dixmude*),
BEFORE THE WAR. IT WAS ONE OF THE
HANDSOMEST HOUSES IN YPRES (*photo,
Antony, Ypres*)

BIEBUYGK HOUSE, AS THE WAR LEFT IT

ST. FRANÇOIS
SCHOOL, RUE
DE DIXMUDE,
BEFORE THE
WAR
(*Photo, Antony
Ypres.*)

ST. FRANÇOIS SCHOOL, AFTER THE GERMAN BOMBARDMENTS

YPRES. THE GRANDE PLACE ON MARKET-DAY, BEFORE THE WAR
(See below. Photo, Antony, Ypres.)

Arriving at the Grande Place, the imposing ruins of the **Nieuwerk** and the **Cloth Hall** are seen on the right.

WHAT THE GERMAN SHELLS LEFT OF IT *(see above)*

YPRES. RUINS OF THE CLOTH HALL, SEEN FROM ST. MARTIN'S CATHEDRAL.
FRAGMENTS OF THE LATTER ARE VISIBLE IN THE FOREGROUND

THE CLOTH HALL AND THE NIEUWERK

The Cloth Hall, containing extensive warehouses, in which the sale of cloth was carried on, was built in the 13th and 14th centuries. It consisted of a series of buildings grouped around a rectangular court. The Hall proper was distinguished from a building called the Nieuwerk, added in the 17th century. The southern building of the hall had a magnificent façade, flanked on the east by the gable of the Nieuwerk and surmounted by a large belfry in the centre. Bold turrets stood at both ends of this façade. Rather spare in ornament, the long succession of glazed and blind windows constituted the grandeur of the façade. On the ground-floor, which was lighted by a row of quatrefoil windows in pointed arches, there were forty-eight rectangular doors.

Above these doors were the high windows of the upper storey, the Hall having two floors. These windows were alternately glazed and blind—a method frequently adopted in the Middle Ages, to avoid weakness in the walls, without detracting from the symmetry of the exterior. This storey was reached by staircases, access to which was gained through doors at each end of the façade.

The glazed windows were decorated with three trefoils supported on two arches. The blind windows were similar to the windows of the ground-floor, except that the latter were less lofty. The two arches formed niches, each of which contained a statue: that of a Count of Flanders (the Counts and Countesses from Baudoin Bras-de-Fer to Charles Quint were represented) or of a notable citizen of Ypres, such as Melchior Broederlam, the painter. These statues, some of which were restored in the 19th century, rested on a corbel apparently supported by a small figure bearing the coat-of-arms of the sovereign represented.

YPRES. THE CLOTH HALL, NIEUWERK AND CATHEDRAL (*in the background*)
*The 13th–14th Hall had a magnificent façade, surmounted by a high bell-tower
(photo, Antony, Ypres).*

The upper portion of the walls was decorated with an ornamental frieze
and a battlement bordered with fine moulding. The frieze was composed of
a tricusped arcade with small columns carried on corbels with carved heads.

Behind the battlements ran a sentry-way, while at the ends of the façade
turrets decorated with arcades and surmounted by octagonal spires, served
as watch-towers.

The Belfry rose from the centre of the buildings, of which it was the
oldest part, the foundation-stone having been laid by Baudoin IX., Count

THE WINDOWS OF THE FIRST STOREY OF THE CLOTH HALL
*Every alternate window was blind, and was ornamented with statues of the Counts
of Flanders or other notable persons of the city (photo, Antony, Ypres).*

of Flanders, in 1201. Square in plan, it consisted of three stories. Its exterior, like that of the façade, was decorated with arches, and was lighted with windows ornamented with trefoils. It had two rows of battlements, four corner-turrets, and a timber-work roof surmounted by a campanile, above which rose a small spire. At the base of this campanile there were four copper eagles, dating from 1330. At the foot of the belfry a door, flanked by two pilasters, led to the inner court of the Hall. Over this door was a modern statue of Nôtre-Dame-de-Tuine, with the Lion of Flanders above.

The belfry served all the purposes of a Hôtel-de-Ville (previous to the 14th century there were no Hôtels-de-Ville properly so-called). It was there

YPRES. ALL THAT REMAINS OF THE FAÇADE OF THE CLOTH HALL

that the representatives of the guilds held their meetings, and that the charters of the guilds were kept in great coffers with manifold locks. There, also, the archives of the town were stored. The bottom storey was used as a prison. From the summit, unceasing watch was kept, to warn the citizens of danger, especially that of fire.

The roof of the Hall was pitched very high, in order the more easily to get rid of snow and rain water. It was gilded and emblazoned with the arms of the city and those of the County of Flanders. This roof, with its dormer windows, did not cover a stone vaulting, but a panelled ceiling. Inside the upper storey were large wainscotted galleries, which, in the 19th century, were divided by partitions and adorned with mural decorations.

PORTAL OF THE
BELL-TOWER

*The collapse of the façade which framed the tower
(photo below) left the latter standing alone. The
lower portion still exists, thanks to its massive
construction (photo, Antony, Ypres).*

THE PORTAL
BEFORE THE
WAR

The Pauwels Room

During the last century, the Hall was frequently restored and embellished. In 1876 the walls of the eastern half of the southern building were decorated with twelve mural paintings by Ferdinand Pauwels, representing the principal events in the history of Ypres, in the days of its prosperity (1187 to the siege by the people of Ghent in 1383). The artist displayed exquisite taste, especially in the fresco depicting the "Wedding of Mahaut de Béthune with Mathias de Lorraine." The western half of the gallery was decorated by the artist Delbecke, with paintings depicting the life of a cloth merchant. Owing to the death of the artist, the last picture was never finished. This gallery was used as a banqueting hall. A number of statues by Puyenbroeck of Brussels, along the southern façade, had replaced the originals, badly damaged during the Revolution (1793).

The River Yperlée formerly flowed past the western façade and, until 1848, there was a flight of steps with a double balustrade (17th century) to facilitate the transfer of merchandise from the boats to the warehouses.

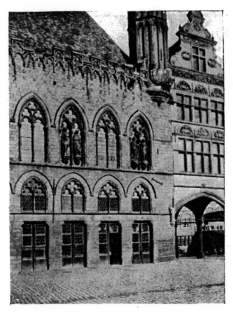

THE JUNCTION OF THE CLOTH HALL WITH THE
NIEUWERK (*photo, Antony, Ypres*)

The Nieuwerk

The Nieuwerk did not detract from the imposing appearance of the southern façade, of which it formed the continuation. Renaissance in style, the plans are said to have been the work of J. Sporeman (about 1575). Building was begun early in the 17th century and finished in 1624.

The ground-floor formed an open hall, 20 feet in width, the vaulting of which was carried on slender cylindrical columns, joined by irregular arcades. The building comprises two stories, the first of which communicated with that of the Cloth Hall. The large high windows of the façades were very close together. The roof was pierced with high and very ornamental dormer-windows.

The Nieuwerk was restored about 1862. In the Chapelle Echevinale, frescoes by Guffens and J. Swerts, and stained-glass was renovated, and at the same time a fine fireplace was built by Malfait of Brussels. Old mural paintings, representing St. Mark and St. John, and a frieze, depicting the Counts of Flanders from 1322 to 1476, were discovered and restored. In the middle of the hall stood a small equestrian statue of John of Brabant (1252–1294) by A. Fiers.

This slightly-built Nieuwerk could not long withstand the bombardment. The south gable, struck on November 21, 1914, collapsed, while on the following day the Cloth Hall burst into flames. A few weeks' later the Nieuwerk was completely destroyed.

THE SHERIFF'S ROOM IN THE NIEUWERK, BEFORE THE WAR (*photo, Antony, Ypres*)

OLD HOUSES WHICH, BEFORE THE WAR, WERE THE PRIDE OF THE
VANDENPEEREBOOM SQUARE (*photo, Antony, Ypres*)

Turn to the right in the Place Vandenpeereboom, formerly an ornamental
pond, now filled in.

Here used to stand a row of old houses with double façade, now completely
destroyed. Here also, to the north of the Cloth Hall, stood the Cathedral
of St. Martin.

ST. MARTIN'S CATHEDRAL

84

ST. MARTIN'S CATHEDRAL AS IT WAS
*In the background: the Cloth Hall. Compare with
photo below (photo, Antony, Ypres).*

The Cathedral of St. Martin

The Church of St. Martin (which became a cathedral in 1559) replaced an older church of the 11th century. Built in the 13th century, its choir dated from 1221, and its nave from the second half of that century. The foundation-stone was laid by Marguerite of Constantinople. The western tower dated only from the 15th century, and replaced a tower which had collapsed in 1433. The new tower was 175 feet in height, and was to have been twice as high. Built from the plans of Martin Untenhove of Malines, it was severe in style.

The plan of the Cathedral was a Latin cross, and terminated in a semicircular choir. It underwent important restorations during the last century.

The façade of the south arm of the transept was of unusually great width.

ST. MARTIN'S CATHEDRAL, AS THE GERMAN SHELLS LEFT IT
In the background : The Cloth Hall.

SOUTH TRANSEPT OF THE CATHEDRAL, BEFORE THE WAR (*photo, Antony, Ypres*)

The central portal was surrounded by a polygonal rose-window and crowned with a high gable flanked by turrets. Above the side portals, the surface of which was decorated with arcading, were gables lighted by rose-windows. This part of the building was probably not earlier than the 14th century.

There were no radial chapels in this great church. A circulating gallery running through the buttresses formed an uninterrupted passage round the building.

At the base of the roof ran an open balustrade, broken at intervals by the pinnacles which crowned the buttresses.

Above the centre of the transept rose a campanile, surmounted by a very pointed timber-work spire.

The nave, and more especially the choir, were remarkable. High pillars with crocketed and foliate capitals supported the springing of the large irregular arches. Above ran a circulating gallery or triforium. The pointed arches of the latter were carried by small columns which originally rested on the wide *abaci* of the capitals, but several of them had been cut away and replaced by statues of apostles, evangelists, or persons of note.

THE CATHEDRAL DOOR
Seen from the interior (photo, André Schelker).

NAVE OF THE CATHEDRAL
(Photo, Antony, Ypres.)
Compare with photo below.

This arrangement is common in Burgundy and, like others to be found in the Cathedral—the exterior circulating gallery, the interior gallery, the form of the latter, and various decorative features — show how strongly French, and especially Burgundian influence preponderated in Flanders during the 14th century.

The choir was disfigured by an ungraceful 16th century altar. The stalls, carved about 1598 by C. Van Hoveke and Urbain Taillebert, were noteworthy, as was also the pulpit —a richly decorated monumental work, at the base of which stood a life-size statue of St. Dominic.

Urbain Taillebert was also the sculptor of the magnificent "Christ Triumphant," suspended between the columns of the main entrance ; and of the tomb of Antoine de Hennin, Bishop of Ypres, who died in 1626. The centre of the tomb represented the bishop in his

NAVE OF THE CATHEDRAL RUINED BY GERMAN SHELLS
Seen from the Choir, near the Porch.

CHOIR OF THE CATHEDRAL
(*Photo, Antony, Ypres.*)
Compare with photo below.

CHOIR OF THE CATHEDRAL AFTER THE GERMAN BOMBARDMENT
Seen from the Porch.   Compare with photo above.

THE CHOIR STALLS OF THE CATHEDRAL, BEFORE THE WAR
(Photo, Antony, Ypres.) See below.

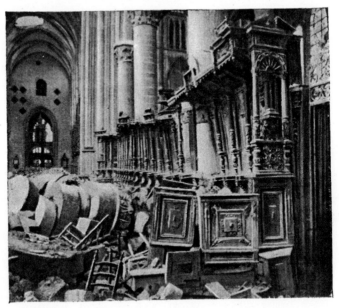

THE CHOIR STALLS OF THE CATHEDRAL IN JANUARY, 1915
(Photo, Antony, Ypres.) See above.

pontifical robes; *on the left*, he was seen
kneeling in prayer, with his mitre close by;
on the right, his patron, St. Anthony, was
represented in a hermit's gown, accompanied
by his traditional pig.

A " Virgin and Child " was fortunately
rescued from the ruins of the Cathedral.
It is a Flemish work of the 16th century.
A surrounding fence (*Hortus conclusus* of
the Litanies) is represented on the pedestal
(photo opposite).

Beside the tomb described above was
that of Jean Visscherius, Bishop of Ypres,
who died in 1613. The bishop, clothed in
his pontifical robes and wearing his mitre,
was represented in a recumbent position, his
head raised on a cushion and supported by
his hand (photo below).

There were other tombs in the church,
notably that of Louise Delage, Lady of
Saillort, widow of the Chancellor of Burgundy, Hugonnet (beheaded in 1477).

In the pavement before the altar was the
third tombstone of the famous *Cornelius
Jansenius*. It was a simple slab of stone, on
which was carved a cross, and in the four
corners the figures 1, 6, 3, 8. Jansenius,
Bishop of Ypres, who died of plague on May 6, 1638, was the founder of the
sect of the Jansenists, which still exists in Holland, and whose headquarters
are at Utrecht. When and how this tombstone was placed there is not
known. It replaced two others removed by ecclesiastical authority in 1655
and 1673 respectively.

Round the chapel, known as the Dean's Chapel, there was a fine copper
railing decorated with small alabaster figures.

The inner doors of the church were magnificently carved; those of the

THE VIRGIN OF ST. MARTIN
(*Photo, Antony, Ypres.*)

MAUSOLEUM OF JEAN VISSCHERIUS
(*Photo, Antony, Ypres.*)

THE MAISON DES BATELIERS (1629)

Completely destroyed. Note the two emblematical ships on the façade. (Photo, Antony, Ypres.)

south portal, with superimposed figures of saints, were considered to be marvels of Belgian art.

In the Place Vandenpeerboom, take the Rue de Boesinghe. Leaving the Rue d'Elverdinighe (see plan, p. 72) *on the left*, the Cattle Market is next reached, formerly a pond, since filled in. Here were three guild-houses, Nos. 15, 19 and 21. No. 15 was the Maison des Bateliers, on whose façade two symbolic boats were depicted. The canal which passed before the house has disappeared. The date of construction was shown by anchors fixed in the wall of the second storey : 1-6-2-9. At the top of the gable there was an involuted niche which probably sheltered the statue of the patron-saint of sailors (photo opposite). The next house, part of which may be seen on the right of the photo, was 17th century.

Take the road on the left which rejoins the Promenade, and turning again to the left, skirt " *La Plaine d'Amour* " (photos below and p. 91). Behind the prison walls there is a British cemetery in the gardens (photo, p. 91).

THE " PLAINE D'AMOUR," WITH YPRES IN THE DISTANCE, DEVASTATED BY THE WAR

Compare with photo opposite.

BRITISH CEMETERY, BEHIND THE PRISON

Turn to the left into the Chaussée de Furnes, leaving on the left the reservoir of the ruined waterworks. *Take Boulevard Malou and return to the Grande Place,* via *the Rue de Stuers and the Rue au Beurre* (photos, p. 92).

THE " PLAINE D'AMOUR," BEFORE THE WAR
See photo opposite. (*Photo, Antony, Ypres.*)

RUE AU BEURRE, BEFORE THE WAR (*photo, Antony, Ypres*)

Pass the ruins of St. Nicolas Church.
Before reaching the Grande Place the site of the Meat Market (photo, p. 93) is passed.

RUE AU BEURRE, DESTROYED BY GERMAN SHELLS

THE MEAT MARKET, BEFORE THE WAR
(*Photo, Antony, Ypres.*)

This was an important, two-gabled building of symmetrical proportions. The lower part of the façade resembled that of the Cloth Hall, but the upper story and roof of the building were of a later date. The gables, with stair-like copings, were decorated with blind windows. The lower storey

THE MEAT MARKET, RUINED BY ENEMY BOMBARDMENTS

THE " HOSPICE BELLE " (WOMEN'S ASYLUM), RUE DE LILLE

was of stone, while the gables and the upper part of the façade were brick.

HOSPICE BELLE, BEFORE THE WAR
(*Photo, Antony, Ypres.*)

The first storey was formerly occupied by the Brotherhood of St. Michael. The Museum, which was housed there, contained a number of pictures, interesting drawings of the old wooden fronts of the houses of Ypres (by L. Boehm). old chests containing the Charters of the Drapers, pieces of sculpture and wrought ironwork.

Almost directly opposite the Cloth Hall is the Rue de Lille, in which, on the right, is the **Hospice Belle** (photos, p. 94).

This asylum for aged women was founded about 1279 by Christine de Guines, widow of Solomon Belle, Lord of Boesinghe, and rebuilt in the 17th century. The façade of the chapel, which faced the Rue de Lille, contained twin doors, surmounted by a large

VAULTING OF THE OLD FRENCH BARRACKS

stained-glass window set in a radiating flamboyant framework. In addition to the statue of St. Nicholas (against the central mullion of the stained-glass window), the lower part of this façade was embellished with statues, in Renaissance niches, of the foundress and her husband. Above the window was an *oculus*, the decoration of which was mingled with that of an escutcheon immediately beneath it, on which the date " 1616 " could still be deciphered.

Inside the chapel were a 17th century portable confessional (a very curious specimen of carved woodwork), 15th century copper candelabra, and a fine picture attributed to Melchior Broederlam. This artist, whose works are very rare, was a native of Ypres. He painted at Dijon about 1380, and preceded J. van Eyck as official painter to the Dukes of Burgundy. This picture was saved.

On the right of the street, in the midst of the ruins, can be seen the broken-in vaulting of the old French Barrack (photo above), and on the left, the **Hôtel Merghelynck.**

The latter charming 18th century house stood at the corner of the Rue des Fripiers. It was built (1774–1776) from the plans of Thomas Gombert of Lille, and its last proprietors had converted it into an interesting museum.

It was decorated with woodwork, panelling, and Louis XVI. medallions by Ant. Jos. de la Dicque.

HÔTEL MERGHELYNCK, BEFORE THE WAR
(Photo, Antony, Ypres.)

THE TEMPLARS' HOUSE IN THE RUE DE LILLE

The stucco ornamentation was the work of Grégoire Joseph Adam of Valenciennes. The staircase balustrading was by Jacques Beernaert.

WOODEN HOUSES IN THE RUE DE LILLE
(Photo, Antony, Ypres.)

ST. PETER'S CHURCH (*photo, Antony, Ypres*)

A white stone vase, carved from designs by Rubens, stood in the fine court of the house.

Almost opposite, at No. 68, was the old 14th century **Templars' House.**

RUINS OF ST. PETER'S CHURCH (*see above*)

ST. PETER'S
CHURCH.
THE CHOIR
(*See below.*)

since turned into a post-office (photo, p. 96). The Church of St. Pierre
is next reached.

ST. PETER'S CHURCH, THE CHOIR BEFORE THE WAR (*photo, Antony, Ypres*)

THE RAMPARTS, LILLE GATE AND ST. PETER'S CHURCH
(*Photo, Antony, Ypres.*) *See below.*

This 11th century church had been largely rebuilt. The façade was surmounted by a substantial square tower, flanked by four corner turrets and crowned by an octagonal spire rebuilt in 1868.

Inside, lofty columns supported the springing of the large irregular arches. There was no vaulting, the church having a timber-work roof in shape of

AFTER FOUR YEARS' BOMBARDMENTS (*see above*)

St. Nicolas   Old French Barracks   School

PANORAMIC VIEW OF THE RUINS
(The point from where this photograph was taken is

an inverted keel. In it were a 16th century altar, large carved pulpit and a fine choir-screen.

Rue de Lille ends at Lille Gate. Before passing through, climb up the

RUINS OF THE HÔTEL DE GAND, RUE DES CHIENS

OF YPRES TAKEN FROM LILLE GATE
shown on the plan on p. 72 (at the bottom, on the right).

ramparts, from which there is a magnificent panorama.

Pass through the Gate, the towers of which date from 1395. There is an interesting view over the wide moats, and of the ancient ramparts (rebuilt by Vauban), which were ruined by shells.

Turn back and re-enter the town by the same way. Beyond the Church of St. Pierre, take the first street on the right as far as the Rue des Chiens, where, on turning to the left, the ruins of the Church St. Jacques, and the shattered façade of the Hôtel de Gand will be seen.

The latter fine house, with double gables dated from the 16th century. The transition from 15th to 16th century style is very marked : on the ground-floor is the irregular arch of the 15th century, while on the first floor the arches are full semi-circles, framing the rectangular bays, whose tmypana

THE HÔTEL DE GAND
(Photo, Antony, Ypres.)

BRITISH CEMETERY AT THE HOSPICE NÔTRE-DAME

are decorated with flamboyant figures. These tympana were added some years later, thus giving the wide 17th century windows, of which the (French) architect of the Hôtel Merghelynck made such happy use (photo, p. 101).

Having reached the Grande-Place, take the Rue de Menin on the right, leaving on the left the ruins of the Hospice Nôtre-Dame. Next take the Menin Road, to visit the Château de Hooge and **Zillebeke.**

MENIN GATE
On leaving Ypres in the direction of Hooge and Zillebeke.

BRITISH CEMETERY JUST OUTSIDE YPRES, ON THE ROAD TO MENIN

Visit to Zillebeke and Hooge
(See Itinerary, p. 47.)

At the Menin Gate leave the Westroosebeke Road on the left, and take he main road to Menin on the right.

On the right, near the last houses, is a British cemetery (photo above). *Before the level-crossing over the Ypres-Roulers railway, take the road to the ight. After passing two further level-crossings, the road descends slightly.*)n the left is a large British cemetery; on the high ground to the right are he remains of the Château, whilst in the distance lies **Zillebeke Pond.**)n the left is another cemetery. *Pass, on the left, the beginning of an*

BRITISH CEMETERY AT ZILLEBEKE

ZILLEBEKE IN 1919

The mound is all that remains of the Church Tower seen in the photo below

ZILLEBEKE, BEFORE THE WAR (*photo, Antony, Ypres*)

BRITISH CEMETERY AT HOOGE

impassable road, which formerly led to the main road from Menin. Go past the ruins of Zillebeke Church, shown in the photographs, p. 104 (before and after the War).

Return by the same road as far as the railway, and turn to the right. A large British cemetery, containing 1,500 to 2,000 graves, will be seen on the western slopes of the Hooge Crest. The site of the village of **Hooge**—marked only by a notice board—is next reached. There is no trace whatever left of the château or of Bellewaarde Lake. It was here that the battles of July 31, 1917, were fought. On June 2, 1917, the first objecti es of the British, in their offersive for the clearing of Ypres, were the Wood and Village of Hooge. They were only taken on July 31, although the château itself was captured in June.

ALL THAT IS LEFT OF HOOGE—THE SIGNBOARD!

HOOGE CHÂTEAU (*photo, Antony, Ypres*)
To-day the site of the castle is barely discernable.

Again lost by the British in April, 1918, these positions were evacuated by the Germans in October.

Follow the road to the top of the crest, where the "tank cemetery," containing fourteen broke-down tanks, lies (photo below).

Now skirt on the right the beginning of **Sanctuary Wood,** beyond which is the strategic Hill 60.

Hill 60 was captured by the Germans in 1914, and retaken by the British in 1915. It was the object of frequent attacks, chiefly the German attack of April 27–28, 1916.

At the place called Veldhoek, opposite Herenthage Wood (full of concrete shelters and tanks), *return to Ypres, entering the town by the Menin Gate.*

TANK CEMETERY
*To the right and left of the road from Ypres to Menin, beyond Hooge,
fourteen tanks lie sunk in the mud.*

From Ypres to Poperinghe

Cross the town by the Grande Place, Rue du Beurre, Rue des Stuers, Boulevard Malou, on the right, and Rue Capron, on the left, coming out at the Chaussée de Poperinghe. On leaving the town pass over the level-crossing.

From Ypres to Vlamertinghe, the road runs through devastated country; here numerous trenches and machine-gun shelters can still be seen.

Take the level-crossing over the Hazebrouck-Ypres railway, then cross the Kemmelbeek by a bridge, still in good condition, and go through **Vlamertinghe.** This village suffered greatly from bombardments. In front of the partly demolished church the road turns to the left.

From Vlamertinghe to Poperinghe the aspect of the country changes completely. The road is shaded by large trees, and there are hop-fields on both sides.

Enter **Poperinghe** *by the Chaussée d'Ypres, continue by the Rue d'Ypres. Passing the Hôtel-des-Postes and the Hôtel-de-Ville, the tourist comes to the Grande Place.*

POPERINGHE : BERTIN PLACE AND CHURCH OF ST. BERTIN

Poperinghe

Poperinghe, a small town of 12,000 inhabitants, is the centre of an agricultural district, where hop-growing is the chief industry.

Of its three churches, two only are interesting from an artistic point of view.

The Church of St. Jean is Romanesque in style, whilst that of St. Bertin contains some remarkable woodwork : the Vérité pulpit, the Dean's confessional, and the roof-loft are masterpieces of the Renaissance period.

In the court of the Hôtel Skindles there is a tombstone dating from 1171.

Old houses are rare in Poperinghe, the town having several times been destroyed during its history.

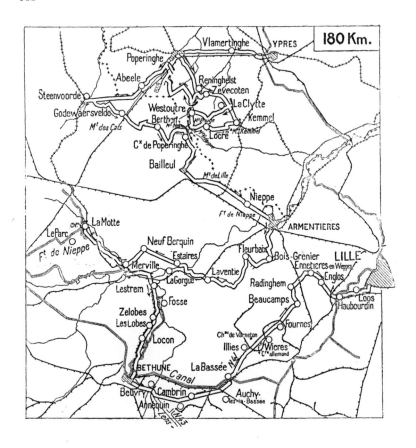

SECOND DAY : POPERINGHE—LILLE

**Via The Hills of Flanders, Armentières, Nieppe Forest,
Merville and Béthune**

Visit to the Hills : Scherpenberg, Vidaigne, Rouge and Kemmel in
Belgium ; and the Mont des Cats and Mont Noir in France.

*At the Grande Place of Poperinghe take Rue Flamande, then Chaussée
de Reninghelst, turn to the left along the Rue des Prêtres, and then turn to
the right into the Rue Boescheppe, opposite the church of St. Bertin.*

Pass in front of the **Diocesan College**, the roof of which was badly
damaged by shell-fire. *In the Place Bertel, turn to the right.*

*Cross the river by a recently restored bridge, then skirt, on the left,
the communal cemetery, where the graves have been destroyed by the shells,
and cross the Hazebrouck-Ypres railway (l. c.).*

LA CLYTTE ROAD AND THE MONT ROUGE

On the left is an Allied cemetery containing 500 to 600 graves. On the right against the sky is **Cats Hill.** Numerous machine-guns shelters can still be seen along the road. *Cross a narrow-gauge railway,* which serves a military station on the right.

The road is first undulat'ng, then descends to **Reninghelst.** *Here leave on the left the church,* which has not greatly suffered. In the churchyard near by, there are a few French soldiers' graves. *At the cross-roads, turn to the left, then 200 yards further on, at* **Zevecoten,** *take the road on the right to* **La Clytte.**

The further we advance the greater the devastation of the ground becomes.

At the first houses of Clytte Hamlet, turn to the right. The German rush of 1918 was broken before this village.

After the capture of Kemmel Hill, a violent enemy attack on April 27 broke down before the desperate resistance of the French 28th Infantry Division (Madelin) and the British 9th Infantry Division.

Kemmel is seen on the left, and **Scherpenberg** in front.

Pass the church (photo, p. 111). *The road turns to the right beyond the*

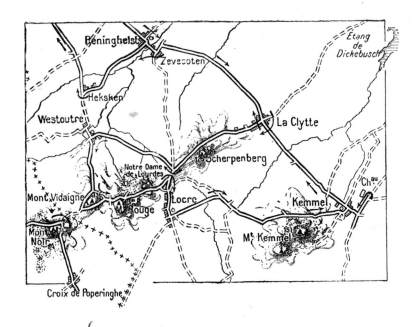

last houses, and gradually climbs the slopes of **Scherpenberg** (altitude, 340 feet). The side of this hill is almost perpendicular, and in it are numerous remains of shelters.

The narrow road which led to the top was completely destroyed. The ascent can, however, be made on foot.

In spite of all their efforts, the Germans failed to reach Scherpenberg in their offensive of 1918. Their efforts to outflank the Flanders Hills on the north broke down before the resistance of the French 39th Infantry Division (Massenet) on April 26, 27 and 28, 1918.

At the next fork turn to the right into the village of **Westoutre.** Here the road winds through the valley. The river on the left has, owing to shell-fire, become a small lake. Westoutre suffered greatly in the bombardments.

Pass the Town Hall, then turn to the left in front of the church. The road rises sharply, and winds round **Vidaigne Hill.** The many shelters in the sides of the hill can plainly be seen.

Behind the hill, leave the road leading to the French frontier, and take on the left the road which first descends and then climbs the slopes of **Rouge Hill.** From the plateau there is a splendid view across the plains.

Leave on the left the ruins of the Chapel of Nôtre-Dame-de-Lourdes.

The road, rising rather stiffly, runs into the Bailleul Road. On turning to the right, the first houses of **Locre** *village are reached.*

RUINS OF LA CLYTTE CHURCH

THE SLOPES OF SCHERPENBERG HILL

VIDAIGNE HILL

Locre was the scene of terrific fighting during the German offensive against the Flanders Hills in 1918. On April 19, 1918, it was taken by the enemy after a daring advance by their Alpine Corps, which had succeeded in reaching Kemmelbeek Valley. On the same day, the soldiers of this picked

RUINS OF LOCRE AND ROUGE HILL

LOCRE ROAD AT KEMMEL AND KEMMEL HILL

KEMMEL CHURCH AND VILLAGE IN RUINS

Photographed from the eastern slopes of Kemmel Hill

RUINS OF KEMMEL CHÂTEAU AND HILL

KEMMEL HILL

Photographed from the road to Kemmel at La Clytte, 500 yards from the latter.

corps continued their advance as far as the crossing with the Westoutre road, 1 kilomètre to the north of Locre ; but here the French dragoons, in an irresistible counter-attack, drove the Germans back and recaptured Locre, leaving only the *Hospice*, to the south-east of the village, in enemy hands.

Beyond the ruins of the church, in the middle of a devastated cemetery, turn to the left; then at the next fork, leaving some French graves on the left, take the road on the right leading to **Kemmel Hill.**

This hill, the first of the Hills of Flanders, is famous for the battles fought there in 1918. On April 17, 1918, the Germans had reached the foot. On the 25th, they rushed to the attack, encircling and capturing the hill, which was held by the French 30th Infantry Regiment. During the next and following days French counter-attacks failed to dislodge the enemy. It was only on August 30 that the Germans evacuated the hill ; on the 31st it was occupied by the British.

Pass Burgrave Farm. At the foot of the hill (inaccessible to vehicles) the road turns to the left. Here the ground is completely churned up, the bits of road being connected up by little bridges thrown across the shell-holes. In the distance is seen the ruined church of Kemmel (photo, p. 113). *On reaching the village, turn to the right, to visit the ruins of the château* (photo, p. 114), *then return to the fork and take the road on the right.*

The road is hilly, as the photograph, taken 500 yards this side of the crossing with the La Clytte road, shows. *Keeping straight along the road by which he came, as far as Zevecoten, the tourist then returns first to the left and then to the right.*

In the centre of **Reninghelst** *village, take the Neuve-Eglise road on the left. At the fork in the road at* **Heksken,** *turn to the right towards* **Poperinghe.** *Cross the river. At the crossing of the road from Poperinghe to Boeschèpe, turn to the left to visit the largest cemetery in this region* (shown on the Itinerary, p. 108), which contains 20,000 to 22,000 graves The photograph gives but a slight idea of the size of it.

FRAGMENT OF CEMETERY CONTAINING 20,000 GRAVES AT BOESCHÈPE.
ON THE ROAD TO POPERINGHE

GENERAL VIEW OF CATS HILL

Retracing his steps the tourizt takes the road which first skirts the railway, and then crosses it (l. c.) to rejoin the Poperinghe-Steenwoorde road. Take the latter on the left. (See Itinerery, p. 108.)

At the hamlet of Abeele there is a Belgian custom-house (visa of " triptyque " or motor-car permit). The French custom-house is at **Steenwoorde** (the third house to the right on entering). Usual formalities.

Opposite the custom office take I. C. 128 on the left, which, after several turnings, leads to **Godewaersteide.** *Leave the village on the left.*

THE CRUCIFIX AND ABBEY OF CATS HILL

CATS HILL ABBEY

DESTRUCTION OF THE CHAPEL CHOIR

THE COURTYARD OF CATS HILL ABBEY AFTER
THE BOMBARDMENTS

On the far side of the level-crossing the road rises, and the Abbey on the top of **Cats Hill** *soon comes into view.*

There is a magnificent view from the wayside-cross on the plateau. Visit the monastery, whose buildings suffered greatly from the bombardments.

Pass in front of the cross and take the second road on the right, which slopes down fairly quickly to the village of **Berthem**, *through which the tourist passes.*

In the hamlet of **Schaexnen**, *opposite the inn with the sign " Au Vieux Schaexnen," turn to the left, passing in front of a small château in the middle of a wood on the right. A plateau—***Noir Hill***—ploughed up by countless shells, is reached shortly afterwards.*

At the fork in the road turn to the right (the road on the left leads back into Belgium).

Go through the hamlet of **La Croix-de-Poperinghe,** *then at the next*

VIDAIGNE HILL AND NOIR HILL

fork take the road to **Bailleul** *on the right. At Bailleul leave the lunatic asylum on the left.* The French custom-house is in the Rue d'Ypres. (In June, 1919, there was as yet no corresponding office at Locre in Belgium.)

Bailleul suffered terribly from the bombardments, most of the houses being destroyed.

Bailleul was taken by three German divisions on April 15, 1918, as well as Little Hill and the Ravelsberg, to the west of the town. But the next day the German forces, who had orders to consolidate their success and turn the chain of hills from the south, were rudely checked by French divisions, rushed up to relieve their British comrades, and in three days, thanks to the prompt and vigorous action of General Pétain, they were driven back.

Have a look round the Grande Place before taking the Rue de Lille (N. 42) on the left. At the Noveau-Monde cross-roads, where there is an important munitions depôt with railway-station, turn sharply to the left, leaving Lille Hill on the left.

After twice crossing the railway (l. c.) the Customs Barracks are passed. The road passes over three more level-crossings, skirts the frontier, crosses the railway, and then the Stilbecque stream. *Next pass through* **Nieppe** village—almost entirely demolished ; *then over the railway (l. c.). Cross the Lys by the Nieppe Bridge and enter* **Armentières,** *via the Rue de Nieppe.*

At the cross-roads take Rue Nationale on the right, and follow the tramlines as far as the crossing of Rue de Lille with Rue de Marle. Take the latter to the right, and cross the railway (l. c.).

For particulars concerning Armentières, see pp. 49-55, first Itinerary.

Keep straight to **Bois-Grenier,** *turning to the right in front of the ruined church.*

Outside the village take the second road on the right to **Fleurbaix.**

Pass the church, of which a few walls are still standing (photo below), *then turn to the left beyond the Square into Rue de Quesnes.* Numerous concrete shelters were built inside the houses.

Near the British cemetery the road turns to the right, then to the left, and enters **Laventie.** *Turn to the right in the Place de l'Eglise, then to the left over a level-crossing near the station.*

DESTROYED CHURCH OF FLEURBAIX

LAVENTIE CHURCH, RUINED BY THE BOMBARDMENTS

After several turnings the road runs past a small ruined chapel, crosses a river, then turns to the right, and crosses the Lys. At the first houses of **Estaires,** *100 yards beyond the bridge, turn to the left, amid the ruins.*

Pass the ruined gasworks and follow the main street shown in the photo below. In the middle ground of this photograph are seen the walls of the church, the steeple of which has fallen in

ALL THAT REMAINS OF THE MAIN STREET OF ESTAIRES

MERVILLE (*from old engraving*)

Leave on the left the Square, in which formerly stood the Hôtel-de-Ville ; its ruined belfry is now a mere heap of bricks and stones.

Beyond a German cemetery on the right, pass through **Neuf-Berquin,** *after which, on turning to the left,* **Merville** comes into view.

MERVILLE CHURCH, AS THE GERMAN SHELLS LEFT IT
Seen from the Rue des Trois Prêtres.

122

RUINS OF LESTREM CHURCH

At the entrance is the cemetery, the area of which has been doubled by serried rows of little wooden crosses, each marking a British grave.

If time can be spared (two or three hours) proceed as far as **Nieppe Forest**, keeping straight on, and leaving Merville on the left.

LESTREM CHÂTEAU
(*Destroyed by the German bombardments.*)

REMAINS OF LOCON VILLAGE

Contrarily to other forests in the battle area, Nieppe Forest did not suffer greatly, although, like the others, it concealed munitions and stores. (Note the numerous narrow-gauge rails lying along the roadside.)

The roads themselves bear traces of hastily constructed defence-works.

On the left, near the outskirts of the forest, a pathway leads to a cemetery containing British soldiers' graves.

La Motte-au-Bois, lying in a clearing, suffered little. Its 17th century château, which escaped destruction, can be reached by crossing the canal over a temporary bridge, leaving on the right a small octagonal chapel of no special interest.

Return by the same road to **Merville,** *and pass through it,* taking a glance at the ruins of the church on the right. *Cross the canal, the Lys, and the railway near the station, and turn to the left immediately afterwards.*

Follow the railway, then re-cross it. The road here runs parallel to the canal. At the next fork leave on the left the road to the Gorgue; turn to the right, cross the railway, and enter **Lestrem.** *Beyond the bridge over the Lawe, pass the church, then turn to the right, and skirt the grounds of an old ruined château.*

This château—completely restored in 1890—was used by the Germans as an observation-post, and subsequently blown up by them on April 10, 1918 (photo, p. 122).

On leaving Lestrem the road winds. On the left, broken fragments of iron-work mark the site of the distillery, which provided a livelihood for part of the working population of **La Fosse** village. The ruined church is seen to the left, on the far side of the canal.

BÉTHUNE. THE CANAL AND SIDING (*Cliché LL.*)

Go through the hamlet of **Zelobes,** which, like that of **Lobes,** was razed to the ground.

Pass through what was **Locon** village (photo, p. 123).

Lawe Canal, after running parallel to the road, turns and cuts it. *Cross the canal by the temporary bridge.*

A little further on, the road again follows the canal as far as the entrance to **Béthune.**

Cross the Aires Canal, pass the railway station on the left, then through the horse-market to the Place de la République. Cross the latter and take the Rue de Rivage to the Grande Place.

For four years the whole district just passed through, since leaving Armentières, was the scene of incessant fighting.

In October, 1914, it saw the close of the fighting which concluded the " race to the sea," and the stabilising of the front here resulted in more than six months' continuous fighting.

A little later, the Artois offensive of 1915 found an echo in local operations for the possession of key positions like Festubert and Neuve-Chapelle, giving rise to sanguinary struggles without decisive result for either side.

Finally, in 1918, it was the scene of the third great German offensive for the conquest of the Hills (see pp. 38–43.)

Béthune

The foundation in 984 of the Collegiate Church of St. Bartholomew, by Robert I., ancestor of Sully, is the first mention of Béthune in history. The town, owned in turn by the Counts of Flanders, the Dukes of·Burgundy, and the House of Austria, annexed to France at the Peace of Nimègue in 1678, taken in 1710 by the Triple Alliance, was finally restored to France in 1713 by the Treaty of Utrecht.

A fraternity, called the "Confrérie des Charitables," still survives. Founded after the plague of 1188 by two blacksmiths, to whom St. Eloi appeared in a vision, asking them to assist their fellow-countrymen who were dying unsuccoured, it performed the burial rites of the dead.

During the Great War the town was intermittently bombarded for three and a half years, but from the end of February, 1918, to April 21 the violence of the shelling increased tenfold, and on the latter date the civil population had to be evacuated, the battle having carried the German lines within two miles of Béthune.

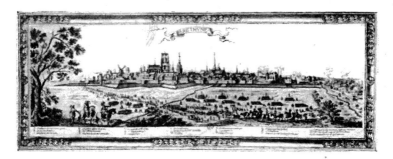

BÉTHUNE, *from an old engraving*

On April 13–18 the bombardment became so intense that the town was almost razed to the ground.

The officials and the miners of the district were mentioned in Orders of the Day for their courage and endurance.

At first sight, the town does not seem to have suffered so much, but this impression soon passes.

The Grande Place (photo, p. 126), where the chief beauties of this small town were concentrated, is now a heap of bricks and stones.

The old houses have fallen in ; only the façade of one of them (No. 44), dating from the 16th century, remains, and even this one was severely damaged and is now supported by wooden props.

Of the modern Hôtel-de-Ville there remains only a small portion of the façade (photo, p. 127), whilst the Savings Bank on the left is a shapeless ruin.

The belfry, built in 1346 and restored forty years later, is still standing,

BÉTHUNE. THE GRANDE PLACE. *Before the War.* (*Cliché LL.*)

but the upper portion of it has disappeared, and the houses which surrounded it have fallen in.

Its tower is standing, as far as the upper part of the sun-dial, whilst the four admirable gargoyles which project at the corners, and the graceful curve of the pointed windows of its first storey, escaped injury.

The remains of the spiral staircase leading to the top may still be seen, but the 15th century wooden spire has gone.

BÉTHUNE. THE GRANDE PLACE. *After the Bombardments*

BÉTHUNE. RUINS OF THE HÔTEL-DE-VILLE

This spire contained a peal of bells, one of which, dated 1576, was called "La Joyeuse."

"La Joyeuse" is silenced for ever.

This peal gave its name to the street behind the belfry, which leads to the Church of St. Waast (1533–1545), whose massive tower was more than half-a-century later than the rest of the building.

To leave the town, return from the Grande Place to the Place de la République (in June, 1917, it was impossible to take the Rue d'Arras, which is the direct road, all this part of the town being obstructed by ruins).

In the Place de la République take the Boulevard Victor-Hugo on the right, and then Rue Marcelin-Berthelot, also on the right. At the cross-roads take the Rue de Lille to the left. The Faubourg de Lille suffered severely from the bombardment. *Take N. 41 alongside the Aire Canal.*

RUINS OF ST. WAAST CHURCH

BÉTHUNE. RUE D'ARRAS, BEFORE
KULTUR'S BLIGHT FELL ON IT.
(*Cliché LL.*) (*See below.*)

BÉTHUNE. RUE D'ARRAS—WHAT THE GERMAN SHELLS LEFT OF IT (*see above*)

DESTROYED BRIDGE ACROSS THE BASSÉE

For four years the fighting never ceased in this region. *Leave the Festubert sector on the right.* Throughout the struggle, the Canadians fought so bravely that one of their recruiting posters was dedicated to the heroes of Festubert, with this inscription :

> " Oui, vous avez raison, c'est hideux le carnage,
> Oui, le progrés blessé recule et se débat,
> Notre siècle en fureur retourne au moyen âge,
> Mais sachons donc nous battre, au moins, puisqu'on se bat."

At the crossing of N. 41 and 43 leave the latter on the right.

Cross the Grande Rue d'Annequin. From here, on the right, coalpit No. 9 can be seen, with its wrecked machinery in the air—a mass of twisted ironwork.

The ruined village of **Cambrin** *is next passed through. On the other side of the level-crossing, leave on the right the badly damaged village of* **Auchy-lez-La-Bassée.** *The road now follows the canal.* After crossing the railway (*l.c.*) vast heaps of broken railway trucks smashed by the shells can be seen in the fields on the right. Further on are eight or nine blockhouses which were formerly brick-kilns. *Turn to the left, cross the railway, then the Aire Canal by the new suspension bridge* (beside the old one shown in the photograph) *and enter* **La Bassée,** *now a heap of ruins.*

La Bassée, an important centre standing at the junction of several roads and railways, in the heart of the plain of Flanders, south-west of Lille, was the objective of many desperate struggles during the war.

In October, 1914, the district of La Bassée was the scene of endless conflicts between the Allied and enemy cavalry forces, the little town finally remaining in the hands of the Germans.

A year later, the British offensive in Artois drove back the Germans south of La Bassée, whilst to the north the positions of Neuve-Chapelle and Aubers were bitterly disputed. However, the lines shifted but little, and La Bassée still remained in the centre of the line of fire.

E

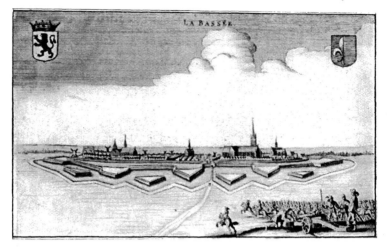

LA BASSÉE, *from an old engraving*

During the German offensive of 1918, the town again came inside the German lines, but the enemy were driven out shortly afterwards, during the Allied offensive that led to the Armistice and to the consummation of victory.

Go through the Rue d'Estaires, in which there is a large and very high armoured shelter that served as an observation-post. *Pass the ruined church* (photo, p. 132), *then turn to the right into the Grande Place.* Inside a three-storied house, which later collapsed under the shell-fire (photo, p. 132), there was a German observation-post of concrete, armed with machine-guns.

On leaving La Bassée continue along N. 41, with its fine trees cut down and left along the sides of the road. *Pass the first houses of* **Illies** *village, on the left, and 100 yards further on, cross a large avenue (leading to the Château de Varneton).*

LA BASSÉE.
STREET
CAMOUFLAGED
BY THE
GERMANS
(*Note the high poles on the left.*)

LA BASSÉE.
RUE
D'ESTAIRES
BEFORE
THE WAR
(*Compare
with
photo
below.*)

On the right, and connected with *N*. 41 by a small bridge, there is a large German cemetery with a monument to the memory of the soldiers of the XVth Regiment (Prinz Friedrich) (photo, p. 133).

The road leads to **Fournes,** *the outskirts of which are crossed by Rue Pasteur.* Pass an avenue of fine trees leading to the Château of Comte d'Hespel, accidentally burned down.

At the cross-roads there is a bandstand erected by the Germans. A crude painting on the back of the stand represents a tug-of-war between a German and British, French and American soldiers, in which the German wins apparently with ease. Italy, depicted as a monkey, is seen clinging to the rope.

After turning to the right the road passes the large Gambert Boarding School, which was severely damaged. Behind it is a large cemetery.

Follow the road to the badly damaged village of **Beaucamps,** where there are numerous concrete shelters in the houses. *At the cross-roads turn to the left.* A wayside-cross, ten yards further on, indicate the road. A short distance further on are the ruins of the Château de Flandre, the basement of which, in reinforced concrete, was used as a machine-gun emplacement.

LA BASSÉE.
RUE
D'ESTAIRES
IN 1919
(*Compare with
photo above.*)

LA BASSÉE. ALL THAT REMAINS OF THE CHURCH

The tourist next comes to what was **Radinghem.** *Beyond the ruined church (photo, p. 133), turn to the right past an armoured shelter, which defended the road, pass under the railway, and at the hamlet of* **La Vallée,** *beyond a chapel, turn to the right into* **Ennetières.** *The road continues through the ruins of* **Englos** *and* **Haubourdin.**

LA BASSÉE. CONCRETE OBSERVATION-POST BUILT BY THE GERMANS
INSIDE A HOUSE WHICH, LATER, COLLAPSED

GERMAN CEMETERY
ON THE RIGHT
OF THE ROAD.
FROM LA BASSÉE TO
TOURNES, 100 YDS.
FROM ILLIES. (*See
Itinerary, p.* 108.)

GERMAN FUNEREAL MONUMENT

Haubourdin suffered comparatively little from the shells, but like all the other occupied towns of France, it was subjected to exactions, war-levies, deportations and pillage.   The German soldiers, when relieved from the Hindenburg line, had their rest-billets there.   The church (of no especial interest), the hospital (15th century), and a chapel built in 1347, are still preserved.

After passing through **Loos,** *return to* **Lille,** *entering by the Béthune Gate.*

RADINGHEM IN RUINS

LILLE. THE EX-KAISER IN THE PLACE CORMONTAIGNE

For visiting Lille, see the Michelin Illustrated Guide : " Lille Before and During the War."

LILLE. THE COURTYARD OF THE BOURSE, WITH BRONZE STATUE OF NAPOLEON I.
CAST FROM CANNONS CAPTURED AT AUSTERLITZ

THE COLLAPSE OF A HOUSE ON THE RUE DE PARIS

LILLE. ENTRY OF THE BRITISH 5TH ARMY ON OCT. 21, 1918

KEMMEL HILL
Seen from the road to Warneton, at Neuve Eglise.

THE BRITISH FORCES
ENGAGED
in the
YPRES
SECTOR

VISCOUNT FRENCH OF YPRES,
K.P., G.C.B., O.M., G.C.V.O., K.C.M.G.

The Orders of Battle have been compiled from information supplied by the Historical Section (Military Branch) Committee of Imperial Defence, with permission of the Army Council, War Office.

Commander-in-Chief . . FIELD-MARSHAL SIR JOHN FRENCH.

Photo, F. A. Swaine, London.

FIELD-MARSHAL VISCOUNT ALLENBY, G.C.B., C.M.G.

Cavalry Division . . MAJOR-GEN. SIR E. H. H. ALLENBY.

1st Cav. Bde. : BRIG.-GEN. C. J. BRIGGS. *4th Cav. Bde.*: BRIG.-GEN. THE HON. C. E. BINGHAM.
2nd Cav. Bde. : BRIG.-GEN. H. DE B. DE LISLE. *5th Cav. Bde.* : BRIG.-GEN. SIR P. W. CHETWODE.
3rd Cav. Bde. : BRIG.-GEN. H. DE LA P. GOUGH. *R.H.A.* : BRIG.-GEN. B. F. DRAKE.

FIELD-MARSHAL EARL HAIG,
K.T., G.C.B., O.M., G.C.V.O., K.C.I.E.

Photo, F. A. Swaine, London,
GENERAL SIR H. L. SMITH-DORRIEN,
G.C.B., G.C.M.G., D.S.O.

First Army Corps . . . LIEUT.-GEN. SIR DOUGLAS HAIG.

Brig.-Gen. R.A. : BRIG.-GEN. H. S. HORNE. | *Brig.-Gen. R.E.* : BRIG.-GEN. S. R. RICE.
1st Division, MAJOR-GEN. S. H. LOMAX. | *2nd Division,* MAJOR-GEN. C. C. MUNRO.
1st Guards Bde. : BRIG.-GEN. F. I. MAXSE. | *4th Guards Bde.* : BRIG.-GEN. R. SCOTT-KERR.
2nd Inf. Bde. : BRIG.-GEN. E. S. BULFIN. | *5th Inf. Bde.* : BRIG.-GEN. R. C. B. HAKING.
3rd Inf. Bde. : BRIG.-GEN. H. S. LANDON. | *6th Inf. Bde.* : BRIG.-GEN. R. H. DAVIES.
Artillery : BRIG.-GEN. N. D. FINDLAY. | *Artillery* : BRIG.-GEN. E. M. PERCEVAL.

Second Army Corps . GENERAL SIR H. L. SMITH-DORRIEN.

Brig.-Gen. R.A. : BRIG.-GEN. A. H. SHORT. | *Brig.Gen. R.E.* : BRIG.-GEN. A. E. SANDBACH.
3rd Division, MAJOR-GEN. H. I. W. HAMILTON. | *5th Division,* MAJOR-GEN. SIR C. FERGUSSON, BT.
7th Inf. Bde. : BRIG.-GEN. F. W. N. McCRACKEN. | *13th Inf. Bde.* : BRIG.-GEN. C. J. CUTHBERT.
8th Inf. Bde. : BRIG.-GEN. B. J. C. DORAN. | *14th Inf. Bde.* : BRIG.-GEN. S. P. ROLT.
9th Inf. Bde. : BRIG.-GEN. F. C. SHAW. | *15th Inf. Bde.* : BRIG.-GEN. A. E. W. COUNT GLEICHEN.
Artillery : BRIG.-GEN. F. D. V. WING. | *Artillery* : BRIG.-GEN. J. E. W. HEADLAM.
19th Inf. Bde. : MAJOR-GEN. L. DRUMMOND.

Third Army Corps . . . MAJOR-GEN. W. P. PULTENEY.
(Formed in France, August 31, 1919.)
Brig.-Gen. R.A. : BRIG.-GEN. E. J. PHILLIPS-HORNBY, V.C.
Brig.-Gen. R.E. : BRIG.-GEN. F. M. GLUBB.

4th Division, MAJOR-GEN. T. D'O. SNOW. | *6th Division,* MAJOR-GEN. J. L. KEIR.
| *(Embarked for S. Nazaire, Sept. 8-9, 1914.)*
10th Inf. Bde. : BRIG.-GEN. J A L. HALDANE. | *16th Inf. Bde.* : BRIG.-GEN. E. C. INGOUVILLE-
11th Inf. Bde. : BRIG.-GEN. A. G. HUNTER- | WILLIAMS.
WESTON. | *17th Inf. Bde.* : BRIG.-GEN. W. R. B. DORAN.
12th Inf. Bde. : BRIG.-GEN. H. F. M. WILSON. | *18th Inf. Bde.* : BRIG.-GEN. W. N. CONGREVE, V.C.
Artillery : BRIG.-GEN. G. F. MILNE. | *Artillery* : BRIG.-GEN. W. L. H. PAGET.

FIRST BATTLE OF YPRES.

(October 19—November 21, 1914.)

General Officer Commanding-in-Chief . . FIELD-MARSHAL SIR JOHN FRENCH.

Cavalry Corps . GEN. SIR E. H. H. ALLENBY.

1st Cav. Division: MAJOR-GEN. H. DE B. DE LISLE.
1st Cav. Bde. : BRIG.-GEN. C. J. BRIGGS.
2nd Cav. Bde. : BRIG.-GEN. R. L. MULLENS.

2nd Cav. Division: MAJOR-GEN. H. P. GOUGH.
3rd Cav. Bde. : BRIG.-GEN. J. A. BELL SMYTHE.
4th Cav. Bde. : BRIG.-GEN. C. E. BINGHAM.
5th Cav. Bde. : BRIG.-GEN. P. CHETWODE.

3rd Cav. Division : MAJOR-GEN. J. W. BYNG.
6th Cav. Bde. : BRIG.-GEN. E. MAKINS.
7th Cav. Bde. : BRIG.-GEN. C. M. KAVANAGH.
8th Cav. Bde. : BRIG.-GEN. C. B. BULKELEY-JOHNSON.

Photo, *Russell, London.*

LORD RAWLINSON, G.C.B., G.C.V.O., K.C.M.G., A.D.C.

Photo, *"Daily Mirror" Studios.*

LIEUT.-GEN. SIR H. DE LA P. GOUGH, G.C.M.G., K.C.B., K.C.V.O.

First Army Corps . . . . GEN. SIR D. HAIG.

1st Division : MAJOR-GEN. S. H. LOMAX.
1st Guards Bde.: BRIG.-GEN. C. FITZCLARENCE,
2nd Inf. Bde.: BRIG.-GEN. E. S. BULFIN. [V.C.
3rd Inf. Bde.: BRIG.-GEN. H. J. S. LANDON.
Artillery : BRIG.-GEN. E. A. FANSHAWE.

2nd Division : MAJOR-GEN. C. C. MONRO.
4th Guards Bde. : BRIG.-GEN. LORD CAVAN.
5th Inf. Bde. : COL. C. B. WESTMACOTT.
6th Inf. Bde. : BRIG.-GEN. R. FANSHAWE.
Artillery : BRIG.-GEN. E. M. PERCEVAL.

Second Army Corps . . GEN. SIR H. L. SMITH-DORRIEN.

3rd Division : MAJOR-GEN. C. J. MACKENZIE.
7th Inf. Bde. : BRIG.-GEN. F. W. McCRACKEN.
8th Inf. Bde. : BRIG.-GEN. B. J. C. DORAN,
9th Inf. Bde. : BRIG.-GEN. F. C. SHAW.
Artillery : BRIG.-GEN. A. H. SHORT.

5th Division : MAJOR-GEN. T. N. MORLAND.
13th Inf. Bde. : COL. A. W. MARTYN.
14th Inf. Bde. : BRIG.-GEN. E. S. MAUDE.
15th Inf. Bde. : BRIG.-GEN. A. E. W. COUNT GLEICHEN.
Artillery: BRIG.-GEN. J. E. W. HEADLAM.

Third Army Corps . . . GEN. SIR W. P. PULTENEY.

4th Division: MAJOR-GEN. H. F. M. WILSON.
10th Inf. Bde. : BRIG.-GEN. C. P. A. HULL.
11th Inf. Bde.: BRIG.-GEN. A. HUNTER WESTON.
12th Inf. Bde. : BRIG.-GEN. F. G. ANLEY
Artillery : BRIG.-GEN. G. F. MILNE.

6th Division : MAJOR.-GEN. T. L. KEIR
16th Inf. Bde.: BRIG.-GEN. E. C. INGOUVILLE-WILLIAMS.
17th Inf. Bde.: BRIG.-GEN. W. R. B. DORAN.
18th Inf. Bde. : BRIG.-GEN. W. N. CONGREVE. VC
19th Inf. Bde. : BRIG.-GEN. HON. F. GORDON.
Artillery : BRIG.-GEN. W. H. L. PAGET.

Fourth Army Corps . . LIEUT.-GEN. SIR H. S. RAWLINSON.

7th Division : MAJOR-GEN. T. CAPPER.

20th Inf. Bde.: BRIG.-GEN. H. RUGGLES-BRISE.
21st Inf. Bde. : BRIG.-GEN. H. E. WATTS.

22nd Inf. Bde. : BRIG.-GEN. S. T. B. LAWFORD.
Artillery : BRIG.-GEN. H. K. JACKSON.

Indian Army Corps . . LIEUT.-GEN. SIR J. WILLCOCKS.

3rd (Lahore) Div. : LIEUT.-GEN. H. A. WATKINS.
7th Ind. Bde. : BRIG.-GEN. R. G. EGERTON.
8th Ind. Bde. : MAJOR-GEN. P. M. CARMEDY.
Artillery : BRIG.-GEN. F. E. JOHNSON.

7th (Meerut) Div. : LIEUT.-GEN. C. A. ANDERSON.
19th Ind. Bde. : BRIG.-GEN. C. E. JOHNSON.
20th Ind. Bde. : MAJOR-GEN. H. DU KEARY.
21st Ind. Bde. : BRIG.-GEN. F. MACBEAN.
Artillery : BRIG.-GEN. A. P. SCOTT.

SECOND BATTLE OF YPRES.

(April 22—May 24, 1915.)

General Officer Commanding-in-Chief . FIELD-MARSHAL SIR JOHN FRENCH.

Cavalry Corps . . GEN. SIR E. H. H. ALLENBY.

1st Cav. Div.: MAJOR-GEN. H. DE B. DE LISLE.

2nd Cav. Div.: MAJOR-GEN. C. T. KAVANAGH.

3rd Cav. Div.: MAJOR-GEN. J. W. BYNG.

Second Army . . . . GEN. SIR H. SMITH-DORRIEN.

Second Army Corps . LIEUT.-GEN. SIR C. FERGUSON.

5th Div.: MAJOR-GEN. T. N. MORLAND.

46th Div.: MAJOR-GEN. E. J. MONTAGUE-STUART-WORTLEY.

Fifth Army Corps . LIEUT.-GEN. SIR H. PLUMER.

Photo, Russell, London.

FIELD-MARSHAL LORD PLUMER,
G.C.B., G.C.M.G., G.C.V.O.

Photo, Russell, London.

LIEUT.-GENERAL SIR E. A. H.
ALDERSON, K.C.B.

27th Div.: MAJOR-GEN. T. D'O. SNOW.

28th Div.: MAJOR-GEN. E. S. BULFIN.

Third Army Corps . . GEN. SIR W. P. PULTENEY.

4th Div.: MAJOR-GEN. H. F. M. WILSON.

6th Div.: MAJOR-GEN. T. L. KEIR.

50th Div. (*General Reserve*): MAJOR-GEN. SIR W. F. LINDSAY.

THIRD BATTLE OF YPRES.

(July 31—November 6, 191⁷⁄₆.)

General Officer Commanding-in-Chief . FIELD-MARSHAL SIR DOUGLAS HAIG.

First Army . . . . LIEUT.-GEN. SIR H. S. HORNE.

> 1st *Army Corps:* LIEUT.-GEN A. E. A. HOLLAND.
> 11th *Army Corps:* LIEUT.-GEN. SIR E. C. R. HAKING.
> 13th *Army Corps:* MAJOR-GEN. F. W. N. MCCRACKEN.

Second Army . . . . GENERAL SIR H. C. O. PLUMER.

> 2nd *Army Corps (with 5th Army during Aug.):* LIEUT.-GEN. SIR C. W. JACOB.
> 8th *Army Corps (with 5th Army during Aug. & Sept.):* MAJOR-GEN. SIR A. G. HUNTER-WESTON.
> 9th *Army Corps:* LIEUT.-GEN. A. HAMILTON GORDON.
> 10th *Army Corps:* MAJOR-GEN. SIR T. L. N. MORLAND.
> 1st *Anzac Corps:* LIEUT.-GEN. SIR W. R. BIRDWOOD.
> 2nd *Anzac Corps:* MAJOR-GEN. SIR A. J. GODLEY.

Third Army . . LIEUT.-GEN. THE HON. SIR J. H. G. BYNG.

> 3rd *Army Corps:* LIEUT.-GEN. SIR W. P. PULTENEY.
> 4th *Army Corps:* LIEUT.-GEN. SIR C. L. WOOLLCOMBE.
> 6th *Army Corps:* MAJOR-GEN. J. A. L. HALDANE.
> 17th *Army Corps:* LIEUT.-GEN. SIR C. FERGUSON.

Fourth Army . . GENERAL SIR H. S. RAWLINSON, BART.

> 15th *Army Corps:* MAJOR-GEN. SIR J. P. DU CANE.

Fifth Army . . . LIEUT.-GEN. SIR H. DE LA P. GOUGH.

> 2nd *Army Corps (see 2nd Army):* LIEUT.-GEN. SIR C. W. JACOB.
> 5th *Army Corps:* LIEUT.-GEN. E. A. FANSHAW.
> 8th *Army Corps (see 2nd Army):* MAJOR-GEN. SIR A. G. HUNTER-WESTON.
> 14th *Army Corps:* LIEUT.-GEN LORD CAVAN.
> 18th *Army Corps:* MAJOR-GEN. SIR F. L. MAXSE.
> 19th *Army Corps:* MAJOR-GEN. H. E. WATTS.

New Zealand Division (Unattached): MAJOR-GEN. SIR A. H. RUSSELL.

Canadian Army Corps: LIEUT.-GEN. SIR E. A. H. ALDERSON.

Photo, Russell, London.

LORD BYNG, G.C.B., K.C.M.G.,
M.V.O.

Photo, Chandler, Exeter.

THE EARL OF CAVAN, K.P.,
G.C.M.G., K.C.B.

INDEX TO NAMES OF PLACES MENTIONED IN THIS VOLUME

The figures in heavy type indicate the pages on which there are illustrations.

INDEX (continued).

CONTENTS

.

Printed in the United Kingdom by
Lightning Source UK Ltd., Milton Keynes
142183UK00001B/88/A